MAHLER AND KOHUT

MAHLER AND KOHUT
Perspectives on Development, Psychopathology, and Technique

Edited by
Selma Kramer, M.D.
Salman Akhtar, M.D.

JASON ARONSON INC.
Northvale, New Jersey
London

This book was set in 12 point Bem by Lind Graphics of Upper Saddle River, New Jersey, and printed and bound by Haddon Craftsmen of Scranton, Pennsylvania.

Library of Congress Cataloging-in-Publication Data

Mahler and Kohut : perspectives on development, psychopathology, and
  technique / edited by Selma Kramer, Salman Akhtar.
        p. cm.
     Papers originally presented at the Twenty-fifth Annual Margaret S.
  Mahler Symposium on Child Development held on May 1, 1993, in
  Philadelphia.
     Includes bibliographical references and index.
     ISBN 1-56821-156-2
     1. Self psychology—Congresses.   2. Separation-individuation—
  Congresses.   3. Mahler, Margaret S.—Congresses.   4. Kohut, Heinz—
  Congresses.   5. Psychoanalysis—Congresses.   6. Child psychology—
  Congresses.   I. Kramer, Selma.   II. Akhtar, Salman, 1946-   July
  31-   III. Margaret S. Mahler Symposium on Child Development (25th :
  1993 : Philadelphia, (Pa.))
     [DNLM: 1. Mahler, Margaret S.   2. Kohut, Heinz.   3. Psychoanalytic
  Theory—congresses.   4. Psychoanalysis—methods—congresses—case
  studies.   5. Psychoanalysis—methods—congresses.   6. Child
  Development—congresses.   7. Self Assessment (Psychology)—
  congresses.   WM 460 M2145 1993]
  RC489.S43M34   1994
  616.89'17—dc20
  DNLM/DLC
  for Library of Congress   93-38650

Manufactured in the United States of America. Jason Aronson Inc. offers books and cassettes. For information and catalog write to Jason Aronson Inc., 230 Livingston Street, Northvale, New Jersey 07647.

To the memory of
Margaret S. Mahler
teacher, friend, source of inspiration

Contents

vii

8
An Interactional View of Development,
Pathogenesis and Therapeutic Process:
Complexity and Hazards   **159**
Concluding Reflections on Settlage's,
Wolf's, and Levine's Chapters
Newell Fischer, M.D.

Acknowledgment

The chapters in this book were originally papers presented at the Twenty-fifth Annual Margaret S. Mahler Symposium on Child Development held on May 1, 1993, in Philadelphia. First and foremost, therefore, we wish to express our gratitude to the Margaret S. Mahler Psychiatric Research Foundation. We are also grateful to Troy L. Thompson II, M.D., Chairman, Department of Psychiatry and Human Behavior, Jefferson Medical College, as well as to the Philadelphia Psychoanalytic Institute and Society for their shared sponsorship of this symposium. Many colleagues from the Institute and Society helped during the symposium and we remain grateful to them. Finally, we wish to acknowledge our sincere appreciation of Ms. Gloria Schwartz for her efficient organizational assistance during the symposium and outstanding skills in the preparation of this book's manuscript.

Contributors

Salman Akhtar, M.D.
Professor of Psychiatry, Jefferson Medical College; Training and Supervising Analyst, Philadelphia Psychoanalytic Institute, Philadelphia, Pennsylvania.

Mary Anne Delaney, M.D.
Associate Clinical Professor, Hahnemann University; Director of Child and Adolescent Psychiatry, Hahnemann University, Philadelphia, Pennsylvania.

Newell Fischer, M.D.
Executive Director and Supervising and Training Analyst, Philadelphia Psychoanalytic Institute; Clinical Professor, University of Pennsylvania Medical School, Philadelphia, Pennsylvania.

Selma Kramer, M.D.

Professor of Psychiatry, Jefferson Medical College; Training and Supervising Analyst, Philadelphia Psychoanalytic Institute, Philadelphia, Pennsylvania.

Howard B. Levine, M.D.

Faculty, Boston Psychoanalytic Institute; Faculty, Massachusetts Institute for Psychoanalysis, Boston, Massachusetts.

Calvin E. Settlage, M.D.

Emeritus Training and Supervising Analyst in Adult and Child Analysis, San Francisco Psychoanalytic Institute; Clinical Professor of Psychiatry, University of California, San Francisco, California.

Ernest S. Wolf, M.D.

Supervising and Training Analyst, Chicago Institute for Psychoanalysis; Assistant Professor of Psychiatry, Northwestern University Medical School, Chicago, Illinois.

Thomas Wolman, M.D.

Assistant Clinical Professor of Psychiatry, Jefferson Medical College; Faculty by Invitation, Philadelphia Psychoanalytic Institute, Philadelphia, Pennsylvania.

1

The Influence of Mahler and Kohut on Psychoanalytic Theory and Practice

Selma Kramer, M.D.

This is a difficult chapter for me to write because Margaret Mahler was my teacher in child analysis, my mentor, and later on, my friend. Heinz Kohut, on the other hand, was an esteemed figure seen and known only from a distance. A certain partisanship is therefore unavoidable for me. At the same time, instead of siding with one or the other theoretician/clinician, I would first like to describe their backgrounds and then compare their contributions, especially those pertaining to child development and its lifelong vicissitudes.

THE BACKGROUNDS OF
MAHLER AND KOHUT

Mahler

Mahler was born in Sopron, a small town in western Hungary, a mere forty miles from Vienna. She received her adult and child psychoanalytic training in Vienna. After a brief stint in London, Mahler established herself in New York where she undertook psychoanalytic observational research on infants and toddlers who manifested serious pathology. In an effort to formulate steps in the development of the average child, Mahler initiated a parallel program in which these children, together with their mothers, were observed in a similar fashion.

Mahler had come to psychiatry and psychoanalysis from pediatrics, where her interest had been piqued by encountering children whose development had gone awry. Some from birth had shown an inability to relate to anyone in their environment; they could not form an attachment to the mother who ordinarily is the beacon of orientation. Such children remained in a mechanistic, inanimate, and autistic world. Then there were others who appeared to be developing satisfactorily and relating well to the mother, only to fall apart in the second year of life. In some instances, the latter children, too, regressed to an autistic mental state. These observations (Mahler 1952, 1958, 1965) gradually led her to be interested in issues of identity, development of autonomy, and individuation.

Repeatedly turning to her knowledge of normal development as a reference point for comparison and contrast of pathological phenomena, Mahler expanded her understanding of both areas (Harley and Weil 1979). With this, she also refined her understanding of the autistic and symbiotic phases of infantile development as she had begun to call them. In this context, she now introduced the concept of separation-individuation (Mahler 1967, 1972, 1974, Mahler and Furer 1963, Mahler et al. 1975). She stated that the success or failure of the symbiotic phase promotes or impedes the subsequent individuation process. Of singular importance is the distinction she made between the mother's pathology and that of the child's innate ego deviation, observing that the psychotic child may evoke responses even in the ordinarily devoted mother that are deleterious to his separation and individuation. And again she demonstrated her steadfast allegiance to traditional psychoanalytic concepts when she underscored that the process of individuation is burdened not only by the widening work of reality but by the child's phase-specific psychosexual conflicts.

Mahler, working within the percepts of Freudian psychoanalysis, contributed to, and complemented, the psychoanalytic developmental theory of the first three years of life. Her observations on the second year of life, when, during the rapprochement subphase, the child's psyche is encumbered by continuing conflicts from the oral and especially anal developmental pressures together with early oedipal conflicts, are of particular importance. Mahler did not devise a new technique for psychoanalysis; in fact, she was perturbed by the misuse by some analysts of her concepts as they applied them to variations of technique. Mahler felt that material in an analysis did not accurately represent the actual events of the early verbal, and especially preverbal, times.

Kohut

Kohut was born in Vienna and earned his medical degree there. After a year in England, he arrived in Chicago, where he did his psychoanalytic training and established himself. At first, he was a traditional Freudian analyst. He displayed a "reverential attitude toward Freud . . . [and] . . . a strong idealization of Hartmann" (Kligerman 1993, p. 24). He was well respected, successful, and influential. He served as the President of the American Psychoanalytic Association in 1964. However, gradually his views began to diverge from the mainstream psychoanalytic theory.

Akhtar (1989) notes that Kohut's theorizing can be seen as belonging to three phases: "traditional," "transitional," and "radical." These three phases respectively represent Kohut's staunch Freudian allegiance, the shift in his thinking culminating in the publication of *The Analysis of the Self* (1971), and the full-blown development of self psychology beginning with the publication of *The Restoration of the Self* (1977) and lasting until his death in 1981. Shane and Shane (1993) note that "[by] the time of his death he had developed a unique approach to the theory and technique of psychoanalysis, naming it self psychology, and had established as his central purpose to make of self psychology the super-ordinate framework for encompassing and understanding the entire psychoanalytic process." The Shanes review Kohut's work beginning with his 1957 lecture in which "he asserted his belief that empathy and introspection defined and limited the domain of inquiry in the field . . ." (p. 777). Over the years, he no longer found Freud's drive theory useful. He emphasized frustration as a causative factor in psychopathology (and later applied this view to treatment) and felt that "the self . . . should be viewed as a super-ordinate framework for understanding all pathology . . . This conception placed oedipal pathology and unconscious conflict in a secondary position as related to pathogenesis" (p. 778). The Shanes' article demonstrates that fortunately this narrow view of psychoanalysis is no longer adhered to by many of Kohut's earlier adherents.

Mahler and Kohut

There are many similarities and many differences between Mahler and Kohut. Both were immigrants. Both had had an analytical experience with August Aichhorn in Vienna. Both arrived in the United States after a brief stint in London. Both focused their analytical interest upon the emergence and consolidation of the self within the context of early dyadic relationships. However, Kohut's views evolved from reconstruction, Mahler's mainly from child observation. Kohut rarely acknowledged theoretical predecessors; Mahler almost invariably did so. Kohut moved farther and farther away from the classical drive theory and ego psychology while Mahler remained deeply loyal to these concepts.

Toward each other, their attitudes were ambivalent, an ambivalence more marked in Kohut's case. At one point, he dismissed Mahler's developmental observations as belonging in a sociobiological framework outside "the core area of psychoanalytic metapsychology" (Kohut 1971 p. 219). At another point, he saw each of them as "digging tunnels from different directions into the same area of the mountain" (Kohut 1980). Mahler, too, displayed some ambivalence. She never spoke negatively of Kohut but at the same time cited him infrequently in her writings.

Mahler and Kohut must have personally met, although I have no knowledge of such a meeting. To me, however, it is interesting that in the 1973 list of suggested members of the board of advisors of the Margaret S. Mahler Research Fund of the Mevil Foundation, Kohut's name appears! However, I do not recall his subsequent presence as a member of the research fund.

MAHLER, KOHUT, AND MOTHERS

It is important to note that while Mahler's formulations arose from her psychoanalytic developmental research (together with her experience in child and adult analyses), Kohut's work grew solely from reconstructions in adult analyses. Many of Mahler's and Kohut's expressions and their use of names for concepts they find important are surprisingly similar; however, how they are used in psychoanalysis often is quite different. For example, before 1950, when Mahler came to Philadelphia to teach child analysis, the attitude toward mothers could be characterized as "mother-bashing." The

child's environment was considered to be totally responsible
for the child's problems; this attitude is similar to Kohut's
focus on "deficit." Since "deficit" puts the onus on the parents
who are not sufficiently empathic, it appears that Kohut and
some of his most loyal followers ignore genetic encumbrances
in an infant as well as prenatal, postnatal, and neonatal experiences that may interfere with a child's emotional ability to
thrive, even with the best of mothering (Weil 1970).

Although Kohut speaks of "optimal frustration" as a
necessary prerequisite for transmuting internalization, the impression of many of his readers is that for normal development
to occur, a child must not be frustrated. Kohut portrays the
infant and toddler as passive; this child makes no impression
upon his immediate world. This, of course, is a very different
picture from Mahler's description of the well-enough-
endowed infant who extracts mothering, at times against
considerable odds. Milrod (1982), too, has noted this difference and says that "Kohut's child is a reactive child. He does
not view the child as an active agent. In his theory there is no
mention of a child's active (aggressive) pursuit of independently won identifications even in the face of appropriate
mirroring and idealizing by the self objects" (p. 106).

Faulting the parents for all their child's pains has many
results. Most important of these is that the child's intrapsychic
problems are overlooked and not dealt with. This was very
evident when I taught a child analysis continuous case seminar
in which the class, angry at the mother, was blind to the
child's own problems.

Case 1

Judy was referred for analysis because of her low self-
esteem, pervasive attitude of anger at her siblings and class-
mates, and excessive and unrequitable demands on her mother
and teachers. The candidate treating Judy described her as
"poor and pitiful" and made her sound like Cinderella, dressed

in rags. In truth Judy did wear clothing that no longer fit, often in poor repair, obviously old and faded. There was a massive "seminar countertransference" involving the child's mother, who the participants in the seminar felt expressed her low regard for Judy via the child's clothing. Also, Judy complained of being hungry when she had early morning sessions.

It took considerable energy for me as the instructor of the seminar to insist that the child's appearance might not be the result of maternal neglect, but instead the result of Judy's own intrapsychic conflicts. I have long recognized a countertransference readiness to blame parents for all of the child's problems in some child analysis candidates. This interferes with treating the child, since changing the environment becomes the aim rather than understanding and analyzing the child's intrapsychic conflicts.

Soon thereafter, when Judy's mother came for a regular interview with the doctor, the mother started the session with "I don't know what to do with Judy. Every morning we get into a terrible argument, for she will never wear the new school clothes I have bought for her. She insists on wearing her old, ragged clothes." Careful analysis revealed Judy's dress to be a sign of how she felt about herself: torn, tattered, and dirty (hurt and defiled by masturbation). Later material about sibling rivalry revealed that she feared that wearing new clothes would enable her sisters to wear her hand-me-downs. She also feared that her sisters (and her mother) would envy her if they knew that in her masturbation fantasies she was the oedipal victor.

When, soon after this, Judy announced that she was hungry, the therapist casually asked what she had eaten for breakfast. With no hesitation the child proclaimed "juice, cereal, bacon and eggs, and toast." Her doctor was then able to pursue her "hunger," which arose from her certainty that she was losing out to her better-cared-for little sisters who were better loved than she had ever been.

This case clearly demonstrates the weakness of self psychological approach of readily formulating the surface material into an environmental deficiency model. Careful scrutiny often reveals complex, intraspsychic factors in the child being responsible for the manifest symptomatology. Another problem with the self psychological view of development is the lack of recognition of the growth-promoting role of deprivation, frustration, and even trauma. Self psychology also does not seem to recognize the deleterious effects of parental overindulgence.

Case 2

Jacob came to analysis with me when he was 15 because of his "refusal" to use his excellent intellectual endowment in school. He had the highest I.Q. in his class and the highest PSAT score in his school. Yet he barely passed his courses. He was the eldest of four children in a middle-class professional home. He was imperious with his younger siblings and was annoyed if they made demands of the parents. (They knew better than to make any request of him.) Jacob had few friends, preferring the company of adults with whom he could be very charming.

Jacob had been a much-wanted child of mental health professionals who, from his birth onward, were determined never to frustrate him. His mother hovered over him so that she could heat his bottle before he awoke. She never wanted him to be hungry or uncomfortable. She spoon-fed him until he was 4, stopping at that time because of the needs of the younger children. Thereafter, his father realized that Jacob sat quietly but angrily waiting for his food, never asking for it, even when hungry. In the early school years, Jacob's superior intelligence allowed him to learn without effort. But when the material became more complicated he refused to study, as if insulted that he must do so. He and his teachers engaged in futile battles over his neglecting to do homework assignments. At times he demanded that his parents help, that is, do his assignments.

Jacob was a short, pleasant-looking boy who at first seemed to welcome being in analysis but soon complained of having to come when his mother could not drive him to see me. He chose the children's treatment room over the adult office but did not investigate it, as did most children. He sat and waited. After some time he asked me what I wanted him to do, and was puzzled when I said that he could choose. For quite a while Jacob wondered whether it was better to choose anything or to "just have it given to me." He showed his need to remain passive, to be fed, to not be "inconvenienced."

This conflict appeared in the analysis after I obtained a cup of water from the office lavatory when Jacob had a violent coughing spell. Thereafter, in an aggrieved fashion, Jacob ordered me to obtain his water, often many times. I commented to Jacob, "This is connected with your worries that brought you here." Jacob announced, "My only worries are whether I'll get into college. I'm smart enough; I'll get in." I told him that he must be puzzled for although he had been told how smart he was, he was not doing well in school. I added that I felt that his school problems were connected with his "glass of water" problems. Jacob said wryly, "At least I get what I want, except that my younger sister is taller than I am, and she's not even tall for her age." He sounded as if she were trying to deliberately outdo him; he wished that just wanting to grow could make him taller.

Jacob began to raise an important issue, his delayed puberty. Changing for sports was agonizing, for the other kids were "hairy" and he was "bald." When I asked whether his father had experienced delayed puberty, Jacob was shocked; "I can't ask him anything; he's perfect. If I want to find out about him as a kid my age, . . . well I just shouldn't. I'm not supposed to ask and I'm not supposed to want to know."

There were many secrets that Jacob "was not supposed to know." It was as though, in order to maintain his position of being gratified, Jacob had to deny his curiosity and had to block out from consciousness all concern about paternal adequacy/inadequacy. He had not gone through the inevitable rapprochement-subphase pain of realizing that neither he nor his father were omnipotent. During latency, he had not compared his parents with those of his peers nor had he begun to experience the "second individuation process of adolescence" (Blos 1967). Any threat to his overidealization of parents created anxiety in Jacob. As I carefully pursued this in the analysis, Jacob was able to work at it by saying, "If I know things you'll end my treatment too soon. I won't be able to graduate from high school." I told him that it sounded as though his "knowing" something about me would anger me and afterward I would stop trying to help him.

Finally, he was able to talk about his curiosity. "Knowing" in the transference meant letting himself ask my neighbors all about me, so that he could know my family secrets. I might turn out to be "not so hot after all." His fantasies showed that I might be all good, having no other patients, always giving him what he wanted, or "all bad" by having traits that were quite the opposite. He wanted to find out how many children I had. (If I had more than one, I was a bad parent.) It was much more difficult for Jacob to pursue curiosity about and anger toward his parents, the latter because they had better prepared his siblings to cope with the world, and because they had any other children at all.

Clearly, some frustration is necessry for development. Indeed, it is not the avoidance of frustration but rather the mastery of frustration that builds character.

RECONSTRUCTION VERSUS DEVELOPMENTAL OBSERVATION

Many years ago, while lecturing in New York, Anna Freud said that we analysts like the reconstructed child better than we like the real child. The implication was that we saw the reconstructed child as long suffering at the hands of its parents. The "real child," in contrast brings his own conflicts into the parent–child situation and eventually into the analysis, showing his own contribution to the pathological or painful interactions. In the same vein, I feel that the insistence by Kohut on using material from reconstruction rather than from developmental research, has limited the value of his own constributions to psychoanalytic theory and technique. Fortunately, the attitude of self psychologists toward developmental research is changing. Brandchaft (1977) notes that while some followers of Kohut are reluctant to acknowledge the value of Mahler's developmental research, others are struck by the significance of her observational data. Brandchaft acknowledges the importance of Mahler's concepts "basic trust," "psychic object constancy," the importance of formation of self-object boundaries, the use of drive theory, and others of Mahler's analytic contributions. He recognizes that the child, although necessarily vulnerable, is much less so than portrayed by Kohut. Brandchaft ends his paper with a welcome declaration:

> It is the author's belief that the reconstructions permitted by the analysis of selfobject transferences, together with the perspective of development occurring within a field of interacting subjectivities, afford the possibility of confirming, extending, and amending the historic contributions of Mahler to the further understanding of human psychological development. [p. 175]

CONCLUSION

I hope this brief and admittedly sparsely referenced chapter has demonstrated that in the realm of both developmental theory and technique, Mahler's contributions have a greater allegiance to the classical analytic theory than those of Kohut. Moreover, I hope it has clarified that Mahler did not intend to produce a compendium on psychoanalytic technique. Her great contributions center on development. Many of us have found these developmental findings very useful in our treatment of adults and children. In light of them, we understand better our patients' productions. Therefore, we feel we can treat them more effectively, under the umbrella of Freudian analysis. The contributions of many analysts (Kramer 1980, Kramer and Akhtar 1988, McDevitt 1991, Settlage 1991, 1993) attest to this. And yet, there is value to a dialogue between the perspectives of Mahler and Kohut. From such a dialogue might emerge understandings that have hitherto eluded us. It is my hope that the contributions of Drs. Settlage, Wolf, and Levine and their respective discussions by Drs. Delaney, Akhtar, and Wolman, as well as the concluding commentary by Dr. Fischer, will lay the groundwork for such a continued cross-fertilization of ideas.

REFERENCES

Akhtar, S. (1989). Kohut and Kernberg: a critical comparison. In *Self Psychology: Comparisons and Contrast*, ed. D. W. Dietrick and S. P. Dietrick, pp. 329–362. Hillsdale, NJ: Analytic Press.

Blos, P. (1967). The second individuation process of adolescence. *Psychoanalytic Study of the Child* 22:162–186. New York: International Universities Press.

Brandchaft, B. (1977). Self and object differentiation. In *Self and Object Constancy: Clinical and Theoretical Perspectives*, ed. R. F. Lax, S. Bach, and J. A. Burland, pp. 153–176. New York: Guilford.

Harley, M., and Weil, A. P. (1979). Introduction. In *The Selected Papers of Margaret S. Mahler*, pp. ix–xx. New York: Jason Aronson.

Kligerman, C. (1993). Heinz Kohut and the Chicago Institute. *The American Psychoanalyst*. 27:24–25.

Kohut, H. (1971). *The Analysis of the Self*. New York: International Universities Press
_____ (1977). *The Restoration of the Self*. New York: International Universities Press.
_____ (1980). Reflections. In: *Advances in Self Psychology*, ed. A. Goldberg, pp. 473–554. New York: International Universities Press.

Kramer, S. (1980). The technical significance and application of Mahler's separation and individuation theory. In *Psychoanalytic Explorations of Technique: Discourses on the Theory of Therapy*, ed. H. Blum, pp. 240–262. New York: International Universities Press.

Kramer, S., and Akhtar, S. (1988). The developmental context of internalized preoedipal object relations. *Psychoanalytic Quarterly* 57:547–576.

Mahler, M. S. (1952). On child psychosis and schizophrenia: autistic and symbiotic infantile psychoses. In *The Selected Papers of Margaret S. Mahler*, vol. 1, pp. 131–154. New York: Jason Aronson.

—— (1958). Autism and symbiosis: two extreme disturbances of identity. In *The Selected Papers of Margaret S. Mahler*, vol. 1, pp. 169–182. New York: Jason Aronson.

—— (1965). On early infantile psychosis: the symbiotic and autistic syndrome. In *The Selected Papers of Margaret S. Mahler*, vol. 1, pp. 155–168. New York: Jason Aronson.

—— (1967). On human symbiosis and the vicissitudes of individuation. In *The Selected Papers of Margaret S. Mahler*, vol. 2, pp. 77–98. New York: Jason Aronson.

—— (1972). On the first three subphases of the separation-individuation process. In *The Selected Papers of Margaret S. Mahler*, vol. 2, pp. 119–130. New York: Jason Aronson.

—— (1974). Symbiosis and individuation: the psychological birth of the human infant. In *The Selected Papers of Margaret S. Mahler*, vol. 2, pp. 149–168. New York: Jason Aronson.

Mahler, M. S., and Furer, M. (1963). Thoughts about development and individuation. In *The Selected Papers of Margaret S. Mahler*, vol. 2, pp. 3–20. New York: Jason Aronson.

Mahler, M. S., Pine, F. and Bergman, A. (1975). *The Psychological Birth of the Human Infant*. New York: Basic Books.

McDevitt, J. (1991). Contributions of separation-individuation theory to the understanding of psychopathology during the prelatency years. In *Beyond Symbiotic Orbit: Advances in Separation-Individuation Theory—Essays in Honor of Selma Kramer, M.D.*, ed. S. Akhtar and H. Parens, pp. 153–170. Hillsdale, NJ: Analytic Press.

Milrod, D. (1982). The wished for self-image. *Psychoanalytic Study of the Child* 37:95–120. New Haven, CT: Yale University Press.

Settlage, C. (1991). On the treatment of preoedipal pathology. In *Beyond Symbiotic Orbit: Advances in Separation-Individuation Theory—Essays in Honor of Selma Kramer, M.D.*, ed. S. Akhtar and H. Parens, pp. 351–368. Hillsdale, NJ: Analytic Press.

—— (1993). Therapeutic process and developmental process in the restructuring of object and self constancy. *Journal of the American Psychoanalytic Association* 41:473–492.

Shane, M., and Shane, E. (1993). Self psychology after Kohut: one theory or many. *Journal of the American Psychoanalytic Association* 41:772–798.

Weil, A. P. (1970). The basic core. *Psychoanalytic Study of the Child* 25:442–460. New York: International Universities Press.

2

On the Contribution of Separation–Individuation Theory to Psychoanalysis: Developmental Process, Pathogenesis, Therapeutic Process, and Technique

Calvin F. Settlage, M.D.

My association with Margaret Mahler began in 1950 when I entered the training program in child analysis that she established and conducted at the Philadelphia Psychoanalytic Institute. As a student and then a colleague of Dr. Mahler, I was a close observer of the evolution of her research and her thinking as it became embodied in separation–individuation theory (Mahler 1979a,b, Mahler and Furer 1968, Mahler et al. 1975). As the theory emerged in a series of publications between 1958 and 1970, I undertook exploration of the clinical application of the theory. Subsequently, I and a group of colleagues in San Francisco undertook research on child–parent interaction during the developmentally crucial rapprochement subphase (Settlage, Bemesderfer, et al. 1991, Settlage, Rosenthal, et al. 1990, Settlage, Silver, et al. 1993). It is from this experiential background that I offer my view of the contribution of separation–individuation theory to psychoanalysis.

Separation–individuation theory is a life-span theory of

human development (Panel 1973a,b,c, Settlage, Curtis, et al. 1988). However, its major contribution has been to our understanding of preoedipal development (Settlage 1980a,b). My focus, therefore, will be on preoedipal development, preoedipal pathogenesis, and the treatment of preoedipal pathology (Settlage 1977, 1989, 1991, 1993). My discussion of these topics will include consideration of the developmental and clinical significance of the *appeal cycle,* a finding from the research conducted in San Francisco.

Separation-individuation theory was conceived from research and clinical experience involving Caucasian Americans. Other cultures place different valuations on separateness and independence, and separateness and independence in any culture, including ours, are relative and not absolute. A degree of dependence upon others is usual throughout the life course.

INTRODUCTORY OVERVIEW OF PSYCHOSEXUAL AND SEPARATION-INDIVIDUATION THEORY

Psychosexual theory places drives, particularly the sexual drive, at the center of human development. Drives are seen to be the primary motivating force in development and behavior, with development paralleling the child's progression through the erogenous zones. Progression from one developmental stage to the next entails the loss associated with the child's reluctant renunciation of the drive gratification associated with the preceding stage.

As originally conceived, drives in the infant were expressed internally in what has been described as Freud's closed-circuit baby. However, Freud (1930) later extended the concept of the infant's primary narcissism to include the mother (Loewald 1972). This concept involved the love object in the child's drive development from the very beginning of postnatal life (see also McDevitt 1991). It meant that drive derivatives and affects are expressed, shaped, and regulated within the child–parent interaction.

Freud's (1905) concept of the complemental series also brought in the role of parental influence. But initially the parent was viewed mainly as the object of the drives and the source of drive gratification. The structuring aspect of pre-oedipal development was cast in terms of early ego development and oral and anal characterologic traits. As the term suggests, preoedipal development was regarded as preliminary to oedipal development.

Separation-individuation theory places the primary love object, the mother, in the central position in human development. It posits the innately programmed thrust of individuation as a major motivation of development (Mahler et al. 1975). Although the drives and their regulation—their taming, in Freud's terms—are considered to be major factors in development, they are viewed as relational phenomena. In addition to being a source of drive gratification, the parent functions as a temporary auxiliary ego, an organizing influence, a source of the developing inner sense of security, a contributor to the infant's sense of self, and an object for internalization and identification.

In separation-individuation theory, the loss aspect of development is conceived to involve the stepwise loss of participation of the parent in the child's developing, regulatory, and adaptive processes.

From this overview of Freudian and Mahlerian theory, it can be said that separation-individuation theory brings psychosexual theory into the context of the object relationship. The concept of the sexual and aggressive drives is retained but their role in development and behavior is seen to be shaped within the primary object relationship.

DEVELOPMENT

Separation-individuation theory constitutes a research-derived elaboration and extension of the analytic concept of self-object differentiation. Differentiation involves a sorting out of oneself from the mother in the early process of separation, and the initiation of the process of becoming a unique individual human being. This process is conceived to include further separation-individuation within the later childhood, adolescent, and adult stages of development (Panel 1973a,b,c, Settlage 1992).

An important outcome of self-object differentiation is the establishment of the intrapsychic boundary between self and other. This experience-determined differentiation arises from interaction with the mother, and leads to a conscious, knowing sense of self. It builds upon the innately provided capacities for discrimination between the self and the mother (Stern 1985). Once the intrapsychic boundary is established, further development and therapeutic interaction—in short, being subject to internal change—rest on the individual's willingness to open the boundary to influence by others (Loewald 1970; see Treatment, below).

Early separation-individuation is conceptualized in detail as a preoedipal progression involving the four subphases of differentiation, practicing, rapprochement, and on the way to object constancy. Each developmental advance in the separation-individuation process involves a minimal loss of participation of the parent in the child's regulatory and adaptive processes (Mahler 1961, 1966, Mahler et al. 1975). These successive losses can be emotionally painful and sometimes are resisted. But the loss is counterbalanced by pleasure and satisfaction in the child's new achievement within the developmental progression.

Normally, the loss is accepted and relinquished, by both child and parent, with feelings of sadness and grief in a process like that of mourning. Letting go of the involvement with the parent is enabled by the parallel formation of self-regulatory functions and structures through internalization and identification with the parent. Relinquishment of an aspect of parental participation frees the child for a higher level of object relationship and developmental interaction. In addition, the development of self-regulatory functions and structures diminishes the need for regulatory help and results in increasing independence and autonomy of function in relation to the human environment and to the drives.

The parental contribution to separation-individuation requires love and respect for the child and the child's development (see Loewald 1960). This love and respect sanctions individuation and separation, and does not seriously intrude on the growth of the child's autonomous functioning as reflected in curiosity, exploration, initiative, and the capacity to be effective. The parent is appropriately available to the child emotionally in support of the separation-individuation process. The judicious availability of such support, from the parents or from others, is ongoing throughout childhood and adolescence, and can be important for adult development as well.

Developmental Process

The described understanding of the separation-individuation process led to a conceptualization of developmental process more generally (Settlage, Curtis, et al. 1988). Development through interaction and identification can take place in relationships other than the child–parent relationship. Any developmental relationship embodies a developmental potential or gradient whereby one individual can develop and learn in interaction with the other (Loewald 1960, 1978, Settlage 1980a), as, for example, in a student–mentor, wife–husband, or even listener–lecturer relationship. Developmental process accounts for the formation of psychic functions and structures within each of the successive stages and phases of life-course development.

Developmental process has been characterized as involving the following steps: (1) acceptance of a challenge to develop, (2) a resulting development-promoting tension, (3) developmental conflict, (4) resolution of developmental conflict, (5) acquisition of a new self-regulatory or adaptive capacity, and (6) a consequent change in the self-representation (Settlage, Curtis, et al. 1988).

The presented view of developmental process can be thought of as a detailed elaboration and extension of Freud's (1923) concept "that the character of the ego is a precipitate of abandoned object cathexes." Separation-individuation theory extended Freud's concept to include the formation of the sense of other and of self as represented in object and self constancy.

The Appeal Cycle: A Segment of Developmental Process

The appeal cycle was discovered during research on mother–child interaction designed to operationalize the rapprochement subphase of separation-individuation (Settlage, Bemesderfer, et al. 1991, Settlage, Rosenthal, et al. 1990). The experimental stimulus was separation and its concomitant of separation anxiety, the phase-specific anxiety of the rapprochement subphase. The children in the study were of both sexes and ranged from 14 to 21 months of age.

The semistructured research situation has six phases: (1) parent and child alone together, (2) telephone call to the parent, (3) parent and child alone together, (4) researcher enters room and interviews the parent, (5) parent leaves and interviewer remains, (6) parent returns and interviewer leaves. Each of the phases is 3 to 5 minutes in length except for the interview phase of 25 to 30 minutes.

Over the course of its six phases, the observational situation creates an increasing diminution of parental involvement with the child. This accounts for the phenomenon of the appeal cycle. The research situation involves both libidinal separation, while the child and the parent remain in each other's presence, and physical separation. The data processing focuses on the libidinal separation during the telephone call and the interview. This focus provides a view of ongoing developmental interaction as contrasted with interaction interrupted by physical separation.

The appeal cycle is a natural, regularly occurring phenomenon in both mother–child and father–child interaction (Settlage, Silver, et al. 1993). It is conceived to have four phases: adaptation, distress, appeal, and interaction. In phase 1, the child engages in independent play and exploration, employing the developing self-regulatory and adaptive capacities to conform to the social situation of diminished involvement with the parent. In phase 2, the child shows signs of mounting distress. In phase 3, the child makes either a direct or an indirect appeal to the parent. In a direct appeal, the child seeks engagement with the parent through a direct approach, for example, taking a toy to the parent or going to the parent and gesturing to be picked up. In an indirect appeal, the child behaves in a way that is difficult for the parent to ignore, for example, reaching for the light cord plugged into an electrical outlet. In phase 4, the parent responds to the appeal and the ensuing interaction relieves the child's distress and reestablishes the child's self-regulation. The child then returns to the independent activity of the adaptive phase, and the cycle is repeated.

Developmental Implications

A successful interactional phase is seen to be crucial for normal developmental process: (1) it reestablishes the child's emotional equilibrium by assuaging and regulating the child's feelings; (2) it restitutes the disrupted child–parent relationship; (3) in so doing, it reinforces the formation of the identification-derived functions and structures that are in the process of being developed; (4) it sets the stage for additional developmental interaction; (5) it avoids the excessive arousal in the child of feelings of anxiety and anger, which in turn evoke the pathogenic use of defenses such as splitting, projection, and repression; (6) the assuagement and regulation of anger and the restitution of the loving relationship are critical to the formation and integration of object and self constancy; and (7) the restitution of the relationship provides a model for straightening out any disrupted relationship.

Within the overall progression of separation-individuation, the appeal cycle can be thought of as reflecting a segment of developmental process. It serves development in a number of ways: (1) it is a regulatory interaction initiated by the child but requiring the parent's participation, (2) it operates in place of the child's not yet fully developed capacity for self-regulation, (3) it can be inferred that the parent's participation provides the basis for internalization and identification toward self-regulation, and (4) the threat of loss of relationship and the evoked separation anxiety and anger mobilize defensive behavior. Depending upon the severity of the external and internal threats posed by the loss of relationship and the aroused feelings, the defensive processes can eventuate in normal development and psychic structure formation or in the formation of psychopathology.

Structural Outcomes of
Preoedipal Separation-Individuation

The Processing of Urges and Feelings

The child's urges and feelings are expressed, acknowledged, labeled, and regulated within the child–parent interaction. This processing moves them toward self-regulation and makes the feelings a part of the child's repertoire for monitoring and engaging in relationships. The processing of the child's anger is of particular importance (see Psychopathology, below).

Object Constancy and Self Constancy

Object constancy and self constancy are major structural achievements of preoedipal separation-individuation. Their conception was begun by Hartmann in 1952. They have been characterized as regulatory psychic structures (Settlage 1980a,b, 1989, 1990, 1991, 1993). They result from the internalization of object and self representations derived from the child–parent interaction, including representations of relationships and regulatory interactions. They involve the integration of good and bad experiences derived from the interaction between the primary love object and the developing self. This integration takes place under the aegis of a predominance of loving over angry, hostile feelings (McDevitt 1979).

The constancy structures embody feelings of security and trust in others and oneself, and they serve the regulation of relationships and the sense of self. Although termed structures, they actually constitute a dynamic equilibrium (Loewald 1978, Settlage 1980a). This equilibrium can be temporarily upset by the anger and rage aroused by disruption of an important, trusting relationship. Depending upon the adequacy of the structural integration, the equilibrium may be readily restored or defenses such as projection and splitting may be evoked.

PSYCHOPATHOLOGY

Psychosexual theory places repressed sexual urges and feelings at the center of oedipal psychopathology. But in Freud's

(1940) final summation of the basic tenets of psychoanalysis, he indicated a lack of satisfaction with his understanding of the role of aggression in pathogenesis. His observations had shown that repression seemed to arise invariably from the component instincts of the sexual life. But psychoanalytic theory suggested that the demands of the aggressive instinct should occasion the same kind of repressions and pathological consequences. Referring to this as a gap in theory that could not then be filled, he indicated that it remained to be decided whether the large part sexuality plays in the causation of neuroses is an exclusive one.

In my view, separation-individuation theory places repressed aggressive urges and feelings at the center of preoedipal psychopathology. At the point in the development of psychoanalysis when Freud expressed his dissatisfaction, his focus was on neurosis and its etiology in an unresolved oedipal conflict with symptomatic regression to preoedipal stages of development. He did not have the benefit of our clinical- and research-expanded knowledge of preoedipal development and of preoedipal psychopathology in its own right.

My understanding of preoedipal pathogenesis and psychopathology is derived from the interactional model of development, from research on child development, and from the psychoanalytic treatment of children and adults. The interactional model includes the contribution of both parent and child to pathogenesis. The child's contribution includes the innate givens, such as temperament, tendency toward activity or passivity, affective intensity, anxiety tolerance, and the intelligence and fantasy potential.

My focus on pathogenesis has the intent of emphasizing the *process* of pathologic formation as distinguished from its end result in established psychopathology. This process view suggests and reveals possibilities for prevention of mental and emotional disorders through education about child–parent interaction and through intervention during preoedipal development.

Pathogenic Interaction

The *developmental dilemma* of the human infant is posed by the innate need to individuate and to separate from the parent upon whom one is dependent for survival. The largely experientially determined development of the human infant makes development vulnerable to untoward influence. Because the child needs the parent, the child's regulatory defenses will sacrifice development to sustaining the relationship with the parent. But individuation and separation are not the pathogens. Rather, it is the anxious and angry feelings aroused by the threat of loss of relationship inherent in faulty separation-individuation that evoke the pathological use of psychological defenses. My discussion of pathogenic interaction in terms of parental influences and the child's defensive-adaptive responses has the dual objective of promoting early diagnosis of developmental deviation and enhancing our ability to perceive representations of early experience in the clinical situation.

Parental Influences

One form of influence results from parental *failure to sanction and encourage separation-individuation.* Such a failure perpetuates dependency rather than growth toward autonomy. This kind of parental influence can be shaped by inadequate achievement of separation-individuation during the parent's own development. In consequence, the parent has an intolerance for loss of relationship and a readily mobilized separation anxiety. There is a tendency to hold on to the child.

A second form of influence is *parental difficulty in assuaging*

*and regulating the child's angry feelings and reestablishing a viable
developmental relationship.* Not reestablishing the relationship,
or reestablishing it without dealing with the child's feelings,
shifts the management of the feelings toward pathogenic
defensive operations in the child. The child's attempt at self-
regulation tends to move toward a tight, inflexible, inhibitory
defensive control.

The effective management and regulation of the child's
anger and aggression rest, ideally, on a modulated control of
the parent's own aggression. Such modulation enables appropriate tolerance of the child's aggression and the setting of
firm limits on the child's behavior.

A third kind of parental influence takes the form of *an
excessive need to control the child.* This may reflect the parent's
own lack of modulated self-control. In one form, the need to
control causes the parent to intrude on the child's spontane-
ous, autonomous, appropriately assertive behavior. In another form, the parent takes unnecessarily stringent,
disciplinary action. In still another form, the need to control
causes the parent to withdraw from the child into emotional
unavailability. Cut off from the needed relationship and parental regulatory help, the child is at the mercy of inner
impulses and feelings. Sometimes the impulses and feelings
are expressed in aggressive out-of-control behavior. This can
represent a plea for regulatory help while the defensive formation of pathology is held in abeyance. In a pathological
outcome, the child seeks to regain the relationship by becoming compliant and submissive, achieving this by sub-
verting feelings and impulses.

Under the described pathogenic influences, the child
does not experience the usual parental pleasure in the child's
growth. Instead, the child feels used in the service of the
parent's anxieties and needs. The *right to develop* has been
abrogated (Settlage 1992).

The Child's Defensive-Adaptive Responses

One form of response is *a close identification with the mother*. This response is evoked by the threat of loss as posed by a mother who is inconsistently available. Sometimes she is emotionally available and at other times she is abruptly and inexplicably not available. Unlike the function and structure-building identification associated with normal separation, this identification has the aim of holding on to the relationship with the mother by not individuating and separating from her.

> A 3-year-old boy became preoccupied with girlish activities and insisted on dressing up in his mother's clothes, wearing her jewelry, putting on her perfume and cosmetics, and carrying a purse. At the same time, he showed little or no interest in boyish activities and pursuits.
>
> Beginning at age 18 months, the boy experienced repeated disruptions of his relationship with his mother. She reported that she felt compelled to leave the house. Having made arrangements for a caregiver, she did so, sometimes several times a day. His attempting to become like or identical with the mother served to nullify the threat of separation.

The response of *identification with the aggressor* can be evoked by excessive parental control involving the threatening expression of parental anger and aggression. This defense seeks to overcome danger and feelings of helplessness and vulnerability by becoming like the parent. In denying separateness, it too blocks separation-individuation. In addition, the internalization process is characterized by a predominance of angry aggressive feelings rather than the structurally integrating predominance of loving feelings.

> A 5-year-old boy presented the problem of yelling back at his parents and defying their discipline. During his pre-

oedipal development, the parents, who were in extreme conflict with each other, regularly engaged in intense verbal
arguments in front of the child. This boy's behavior reflected
his attempt to overcome feelings of helplessness and vulnerability.

Closely related to identification with the aggressor are
omnipotence defenses and behavior. They are evoked by feelings of
helplessness and vulnerability during preoedipal development, particularly during the rapprochement subphase of
separation-individuation. These defenses create illusions of
power and invulnerability expressed in grandiose and sometimes defiant behavior that goes beyond similar behavior seen
in normal development.

For several months, a 4-year-old boy came to the treatment sessions wearing, in turn, the costumes of Superman,
Batman, and Captain Hook. In the play activity, he acted as
though he had the strength and power of these fantasy figures.
The boy's father was given to angry outbursts of yelling and
slamming doors when his son did not behave properly, and
also when arguing with the boy's mother. Sometimes he
would storm out of the house, not returning for hours.

Another defensive-adaptive response is that of *precocious
develoment*. Already during the preoedipal phase, some children not only are able to subvert their needs but somehow can
hasten their ego development. Such children may assume
adult-like responsibilities and function as consoler, confidant,
and family peacemaker. To avoid interpersonal conflict, they
become very sensitively attuned to the emotional state of the
parent. Even though they appear not to have been the recip-
ient of adequate parental empathy, they have a capacity for
empathy with others. They are good listeners. Taking care of
others may become a central feature of their later childhood
and adult lives.

The avoidance of interpersonal conflict enables the maintenance of an ongoing relationship with the parent. Although true separation-individuation involving the development of the object and self constancy structures is suspended, the continuing relationship permits interaction and development in the sphere of ego and cognitive development.

Precocious development is achieved at the expense of development of the self and a capacity for intimacy and full object relationship. The deprivation of emotional nurturance and love that results from having leap-frogged over pre-oedipal emotional development leaves a void in the individual's inner life. The structuring of a sound, integrated object and self constancy does not take place. As adult patients, precociously developed children have characterized this void as being without "a center" or "a plumb line."

> In her analysis, a 17-year-old girl revealed that she functioned with what she called her "facade self" (see also Settlage 1990). As she described it, her inner self was a confusion of unintegrated selves: a little girl self, a 40-year-old woman self, a thin self and a fat self, a sexual and an asexual self, a mentor to friends self, and a depressed self. Yet she was very successful scholastically and socially, although incapable of emotional intimacy.
>
> During her early childhood, her father was extremely busy building his career. He provided little emotional support for the patient's mother. The mother became stressed and depressed, and turned to her young daughter for emotional support. The patient became her mother's confidante. She also was the one who eased the family's tensions. She felt deprived of her childhood.

The Appeal Cycle: A Potentially Pathogenic Interaction

A research illustration of a potentially pathogenic child-parent interaction was observed in the case of an 18-month-old boy.

During the interview phase, the child makes a strong direct appeal, tugging on the parent's finger in an attempt to pull the parent out of the interview chair. The parent does not provide a helpful, regulatory response, instead telling the child not to interrupt. The child briefly attempts to adapt but then shifts into motoric, ambitendent approach–avoidance behavior. Distress and anger are evidenced in the child's squashing and biting a foam block. The child now avoids looking at the parent. The looking away and the approach–avoidance behavior intensify into the child's looking at the ceiling with head thrown back while repeatedly rotating his body in a circle, alternately facing toward and away from the parent. The child emits a stifled, high-pitched yell. There is no parental response to this clear, indirect appeal. Appearing disconsolate, and with his back to the parent, the child lays his head on the seat of a chair in front of the one-way mirror. A quick glance at the parent is followed by the child's making faces at himself in the mirror while softly vocalizing to himself. Now drooling, the child squeezes himself behind the back of the chair where he cannot see or be seen by the parent.

If the described kind of experience were to prevail in this boy's life, it seems reasonable to infer that his anger would continue to be defensively blocked from expression. It likely would enter into the formation of an unconscious conflict. If, however, the other parent's interaction with the boy is empathic and helpful, his defensive activity might fall within the limits of normal development.

Repressed Anger and Aggression

Of particular importance in preoedipal pathogenesis and psychopathology are repressed anger and aggression. One effect of repressed anger and aggression is *injury to the sense of self, feeling bad and unworthy of love, with one's needs felt to be unacceptable.*

This effect is illustrated by the case of a 34-year-old woman who suffered from phobias, including a travel phobia (see also Settlage 1991). In a particular session, she indicated that I had not tuned in on her need for help in the previous session. She said that I had assumed that she could handle her anxiety while driving home after the session ended. She did not let me know about the intensity of her feelings. She feared that I would not be able to tolerate them and that our relationship would be jeopardized. She then talked about how she has always been a selfish person.

As reconstructed in the treatment, the lack of response or a frequently negative response to expression of her needs during childhood had made her feel that her needs were unacceptable and bad.

A second effect is *fear of loss of control over repressed, angry, rageful aggression.* Subjectively, the aggression is experienced as a potentially explosive internal liability. Clinical manifestations of the problem of control over aggression include the following: phobias, wherein the internal danger of the repressed aggression is projected away from the self onto the external world; obsessive-compulsive behavior designed to maintain control over the aggression; self-destructive tendencies, such as accident proneness or suicidal ideation or behavior indicating tenuous control; and somatization reactions, such as headache or bowel dysfunction, wherein the angry aggression is channeled into organ systems.

The phobic reactions of the 34-year-old woman with a travel phobia occurred when her anger was aroused and threatened to escape from defensive control. Such arousal would occur in response to interruptions of the treatment relationship. After a two-week interruption of the treatment, the patient reported that she became afraid that her vitamin capsules were poisoned. She indicated that she knew better because she had already taken half of them.

The fear of being poisoned was understood to be a symptomatic expression of her then still unconscious rage at me for "abandoning" her. The rage disrupted the integration of her constancy structures. She attempted to preserve me as a good internal object by projecting the rage onto the outside world in the form of the fantasy of being poisoned.

A third effect is *fear of the powerful combination of repressed rage and omnipotence fantasies.* This combination can be highly resistant to access in treatment. Sensing and fearing the internal destructive potential, the patient is loath to become consciously aware of these feelings and fantasies.

Illustration of this third effect is taken from the analysis of a 29-year-old man. The illustrative material is from the patient's dreams. In the first dream of the analysis, he has a malignant tumor buried deeply in his bowels. In the analysis, this became understood as representing his repressed rage and aggression. In a dream during the termination phase, the patient has an easy, satisfying, normal bowel movement. This was understood to reflect the resolution of repressed rage and aggression.

The omnipotence fantasies were represented in a series of dreams about presidents of the United States. These dreams were widely spaced over the course of the analysis. The patient only gradually was able to see any connection between the dreams and himself. In the first such dream, the president is giving a speech from the podium of a meeting room. From behind a curtain in the back of the room, an unidentified man takes a rifle shot at the president. In the second dream of the series, the patient is a guest at the White House. In the third dream, he is at the White House in an advisory capacity to the president. Early during the termination phase, the fourth dream presented the president as just an ordinary person, sort of whittled down to size. In the final dream of the series, the patient and the president have a very friendly, intimate relationship.

The patient's preoedipal years were fraught with object loss. His natural father abandoned the marriage when the patient was born. The patient and his mother lived with the maternal grandparents. Toward the end of the first year, he and his mother left the grandparents' home. The mother went to work, leaving the patient in the daytime care of her 19-year-old sister. This caregiving aunt left when the patient was 2 years old. His mother remarried when the patient was 3 years old. He experienced the remarriage as still another loss involving sharing his mother with the stepfather.

The transference, the therapeutic process, and the analyst–patient relationship evolved in parallel with the patient's dreams. His intense resistance to the exposure of the rage and to owning the omnipotence fantasies made the analysis difficult and long.

As a fourth effect, *the omnipresent, readily triggered, repressed anger and rage interfere with structural integration.* The rage tends to wipe out positive experience in relationships and maintain a predominance of angry over loving feelings. Good experience fails to "stick to the ribs" of psychic structure and does not serve its usual integrative function. As a consequence, object and self constancy are tenuously structured and have a fragile equilibrium.

A 30-year-old woman and I had had a long and generally fruitful therapeutic association. Nevertheless, relatively small failures of empathy or understanding on my part would trigger rage and defensive splitting whereby I became a totally bad object. The patient would angrily threaten to break off the relationship.

We both were puzzled by this phenomenon. In her attempt to explain why our long association had not resulted in a greater sense of trust in me and a more stable emotional equilibrium, she employed the metaphor of hurling a handful of mud at a wall. She said that what she takes in from her good

experience with me, or for that matter from others, is like the
mud on the wall. "It sticks briefly and then falls off."

For her, structural integration began after her repressed
rage was fully expressed in the transference. An example was a
session in which she glared at me with an affectively intense
"look that could kill." As she came toward me at the end of the
session to leave by the exit door, I unconsciously stepped
backward. I realized that I was taking myself out of the range
of her fist. She expressed her rage and I was intimidated by it.
But she did not attack me physically and our relationship
survived the expression of her rage. As the working-through
process proceeded, her anger was brought under ego modulation and its disruptive effect on structural integration was
alleviated.

TREATMENT

More than 30 years ago, Hans Loewald (1960) brought
development into the analytic relationship by drawing a per-
suasive analogy between the psychoanalytic and the developmental situations (Settlage 1992). At about the same time, Leo
Stone (1961) perceived the psychoanalytic situation to represent the basic separation experience in the child's relationship
to the mother, and the analyst to represent the mother of
separation.

In agreement with these views, I offer a further expli-
cation of the *developmental aspect* of the psychoanalytic
relationship. My view of this aspect is influenced by my
understanding of separation-individuation as an interactional
developmental process. The developmental aspect bears
on psychoanalytic technique and the process of structural
change. I believe that it complements the psychoanalytic
method as traditionally conceived.

From this developmental perspective, the patient and the
analyst confront the transferences of a developmental rela-

tionship "gone awry." They encounter both pathology and developmental arrest. Because the patient seeks to resolve both, the analyst is placed in the position of being both a transference object and a developmental object (Settlage 1993).

The *undoing of pathology* is the province of psychoanalytic technique and therapeutic process as they embrace the basic concepts and principles of the psychoanalytic method: the dynamic unconscious, intrapsychic conflict, compromise formation, unconscious resistance, transference, transference interpretation, and working through. It is the therapeutic undoing of pathology that opens up the mental system to resumption of development in the pathology-closed areas (Emde 1980, Settlage 1980a, 1992, Settlage, Curtis, et al. 1988). *Development in the psychoanalytic situation* is the province of developmental process as it rests on the interaction between the patient and the analyst.

The Interactional Developmental Model

Viewing the psychoanalytic relationship from the perspective of the interactional, developmental model adds a new dimension to that of the traditional, noninteractional model geared only to the resolution of pathology. This new dimension includes the following propositions:

1. Alongside relief of suffering and drive gratification, resumption of development is a basic motivation for treatment.
2. In analogy to the positon of the parent in child development, the analyst represents an organizing influence; a temporary auxiliary ego; empathic understanding; a safe and secure relationship; respect and support for the patient's need for initiative, agency, and autonomy; affirmation of the ex-

isting and emerging healthy sense of self; and an object for identification.

3. Alongside the negative transference, there is a positive developmental transference expressive of unmet developmental needs.

> Developmental transference is illustrated by the case of a 45-year-old man. During his early childhood, he experienced his father as an unloving, hateful man. The patient essentially was unable to use his father as a developmental object. Throughout his life, he sought a father-figure mentor. He brought his developmental transference to the analysis.
>
> The analyst's dual role as a transference object and a developmental object is illustrated by the corrective emotional experience in its nonpejorative conceptualization, as opposed to the conceptualization involving manipulation of the transference (Alexander and French 1946). By behaving differently from the parent of childhood and not reinforcing the transference expectations, the analyst is furthering the undoing of pathology. At the same time, the different behavior makes the analyst suitable for developmental identification.

4. Transference interpretation increasingly reveals the analyst as a new and different object than the parent (Loewald 1960).

5. Where development is needed, the patient can use the analyst as a developmental object. Developmental use of the analyst is qua analyst. The analyst does not assume the role of a parent.

6. Therapeutic process and developmental process are complementary and proceed hand-in-hand.

> With each undoing of some aspect of pathology, there is the opportunity for development in that same area. With each increment of development, the personality structure is strengthened. The strengthened structure increases the pa-

tient's tolerance for the therapeutic exposure of repressed, anxiety-creating urges, fantasies, and feelings. Further therapeutic work is followed in turn by more development, and so on. [Settlage 1992, p. 355]

Because of the close interplay of therapeutic process and developmental process, they are not readily discerned as separate processes in the psychoanalytic situation. Heuristically, however, the postulation of two different processes of change allows the basic psychoanalytic method and therapeutic process to stand as performing their long-standing function of undoing psychopathology rather than being conceived to include developmental process (Settlage 1992).

About a year into his analysis, a 49-year-old man notes that he is listening to and understanding others in a new and empathically understanding way. This is a distinct change from his past behavior. He attributes the change to having experienced how the analyst listens and tries to understand him. He then reveals the new information that he has always seen himself as being mean, relentlessly confrontative, and sadistic in his dealings with others. It is my understanding that the beginning development of his new capacity, in part through identification with the analyst, improved the sense of self and enabled the patient to reveal and begin to address the reasons for his sadistic behavior.

The Developmental Stance

The developmental stance (Settlage 1992) is epitomized by a statement from Loewald (1960 p. 20): "Being an analyst requires an objectivity and neutrality the essence of which is love and respect for the individual and for individual development." Loewald also expanded Freud's metaphor of the analyst as sculptor to include development: "In analysis we bring out the true form by taking away the neurotic distortions. However, as in sculpture, we must have, if only in rudiments, an image of that which needs to be brought into its own" (p. 18).

Like the sculptor who can visualize the figure to be released from a block of marble, the analyst sees beyond the patient's defensively determined character and behavior to the inner individual who can come into being. In analogy to the removal of the image-obscuring marble, the analyst removes pathology. But the analyst also releases a developmental potential. He does so by establishing a developmental relationship, by expecting development, by encouraging the patient's developmental initiatives, and by acknowledging developmental achievements.

The developmental stance includes adoption of a generative position. This places it at variance with some of the principles of the traditional psychoanalytic method (Settlage 1992). But the behavior of the analyst who adopts this stance is governed by the usual psychoanalytic ethic.

The generative position (Erikson 1950) is analagous to but not the same as the position of the parent. The analyst does not bear parental responsibility for the patient and does not parent the patient. But the psychoanalytic generative position does seek to further the patient's development. It involves the maintenance of the gap or gradient (Loewald 1960) across which both developmental and therapeutic interaction take place. This gradient exists between parent and child, between teacher and student, and between analyst and patient.

Maintaining the gradient in the psychoanalytic situation includes not injecting the analyst's own conflicts and fantasies into the interaction, and analyzing rather than manipulating or reacting to and reinforcing the transference. The analyst's participation in the interaction is a disciplined one attuned and geared to the patient's therapeutic and developmental needs.

The psychoanalytic ethic also bears comparison with the position of the parent. The taboo, including the incest taboo, against the parent's exploitation of the child for the parent's own ends is matched by the taboo against the analyst's exploitation of the patient for the analyst's own ends. Breaching this taboo destroys the developmental and the therapeutic potential. Maintenance of the psychoanalytic ethic is essential for creation of the conditions of trust and safety under which the patient is able to open the intrapsychic boundaries—the boundaries between self and other and between conscious and unconscious—to treatment and development.

The Appeal Cycle: Implications for Treatment

The appeal cycle offers insights into the relational and regulatory conditions that govern development. Similar conditions apply to the psychoanalytic relationship. The appeal cycle also offers insights into preoedipal psychopathology in its own right, into preoedipal transferences, and into the developmental aspects of the analyst–patient interaction.

These insights are suggested by the described potential pathogenic interaction observed in the research situation (see above). Deviation from the paradigmatic appeal cycle (Settlage, Bemesderfer, et al. 1991) can lead to the formation of pathology and to preoedipal transference in the psychoanalytic situation. And the relationship-restituting and development-serving parental functioning in the appeal cycle suggests the desirability of similar functioning on the part of the analyst in furthering therapeutic and developmental interaction. Examples of such functioning are included in the following discussion of *principles of technique* (see also Settlage 1992). These principles are drawn from comparison of experience in the treatment situation with appeal cycle observations.

Principles of Technique

Actively Engaging the Analytic Relationship

The resumption in analysis of separation-individuation, and the internalization of positive experience that it entails, require the analyst to be empathically and emotionally available to the patient. The patient's experience of the analyst's qualities as a human being is an essential part of the therapeutic and developmental processes. Anonymity about the analyst's personal life is maintained but anonymity as a human being is not.

This illustration is taken from the case of a 52-year-old woman. She returned to see me about a year after the termination of her analysis. Sitting across from me she expressed her feelings of loss and sadness over the impending cancerous death of her husband. My eyes inadvertently teared. Her response was to say that my tears confirmed that I really do care about her.

As I understand it, this confirmation would add further strength to the structural integration of her object and self constancy, as they had been strengthened during the analysis.

Engaging the relationship evokes the transference fears and wishes about entering a relationship. The pathology that began to form in the context of external, interpersonal conflict in the child–parent relationship, and became elaborated and represented internally as intrapsychic conflict, is reexternalized and reenacted in the transference where the original pathogenic experiences can be understood and interpreted.

Illustration is from the case of a 42-year-old man. He had a prior, partially successful analysis. At this point in the treatment, he is not on the couch. His eyes teared as he expressed his grief at the death of his beloved dog. I verbalized that I knew how painful his loss was. With a tinge of annoyance, he said, "Analysts are not supposed to say things like that."

He became aware that my comment had made him feel closer to me. But he was afraid of getting close. He noted further that he had felt quite safe from the danger of closeness with his former analyst who carefully adhered to traditional psychoanalytic technique.

Expressing Empathy Affectively and Verbally

The analyst's empathy with the patient is implicit in any good transference interpretation. For some patients, though, empathy needs to be explicitly conveyed, affectively and verbally. Experiencing the analyst's empathy is a necessary factor in the patient's emotional conviction about the correctness of the analyst's understanding. In addition, when feelings were not processed in the developmental relationship, the analyst's expression of empathy in resonance with, and in reaction to, the patient's feelings can serve the processing of feelings in the analytic relationship.

> During the treatment of a 30-year-old woman, I had interpreted her fear that expressing her anger toward me would destroy our relationship. She said, "Maybe so, but I am not sufficiently in touch with my anger to know that. Besides, it is not enough for you to tell me that. You need to point out my feeling, label it, tell me it is a normal human feeling, and say how it makes you feel."
>
> During her early childhood, there was a failure to process her feelings. Reconstruction indicated that the patient's mother had a fear of loss of control and an extremely low threshold for anxiety. The mother would become distressed and angry whenever the patient expressed her own upset feelings. As a child, the patient adapted to her mother by not expressing her feelings. Accordingly, she did not learn about them and their dimensions or learn how to modulate them.

Recognizing and Analyzing the Power of Libidinal and Physical Separations to Evoke Preoedipal Transferences

Reactions to separations and disruptions of the analytic relationship reflect problems in separation-individuation.

Early in his analysis, a 40-year-old man and I are facing a one-week interruption of the treatment. He asks to sit in the chair instead of lie on the couch. He angles the chair away from a direct vis-à-vis position and does not look at me. He said that he felt I was not with him in the previous session. Exploration failed to reveal any clear-cut reason for this feeling.

I asked whether this feeling and his moving to the chair might be related to the pending interruption of our relationship. He reflected for a bit and then presented associations having to do with the repeatedly on-again, off-again nature of his childhood relationship with both of his parents.

Respecting the Patient's Need for Control Over the Intrapsychic Boundaries Between Self and Other, and Between Conscious and Unconscious Processes

Unempathically timed confrontative and interpretative intrusions on these boundaries tend to unduly disrupt the patient's emotional equilibrium. Empathically assured safety from such intrusion helps enable the patient to open these boundaries to developmental and therapeutic interaction. If these boundaries are transgressed, no matter how unintentionally, the reasons for the intrusion and the reactions to it need to be explored and the relationship restituted.

Over the course of her analysis, a 50-year-old woman gradually felt closer to me but still feared closeness. The fear of emotional intimacy was also evident in her relationship with her husband and her children. In a particular session, she expressed her frequently repeated view that I, like all men, was against women and wanted to keep them in a subservient position. I said that I thought she might be expressing this complaint just because she was feeling more trusting of me, and this made her anxious. I added that she in fact had experienced me as sanctioning her growth toward maturity and independence. In the next session, she said that I was "pompous and authoritative!" Who was I to sanction her growth? I reacted defensively. She told me that I was being defensive and that this clearly was my problem, not hers.

I realized that my defensive reaction was because her remark caught me off guard. I was feeling warmly disposed toward her when I interpreted her complaint. I decided to share this understanding with her. After some reflection, and with much emotion, she said that my making it explicit that I was for her growth had made her feel closer to me. But it also caught her off guard. She dealt with my unanticipated transgression of her boundary, and the anxiety it aroused, by attacking me verbally in order to put distance between us. The ensuing exchange put our relationship back on track.

Acknowledging and Taking Responsibility for Disruptions of the Relationship Caused by Failures on the Part of the Analyst

Acknowledging and taking responsibility for failures of empathy, understanding, and technique confirm the appropriateness of the patient's feelings in reaction to such failures and restitutes the disrupted relationship.

A 48-year-old woman was prone to headaches and would develop them during the treatment sessions. The analysis eventually revealed that the headaches developed when she was angry but did not express her anger. At first she was not even aware of being angry. The emergence of a headache during a session was a clear sign that she was angry at me because I had failed to understand her or had said something that she did not like or could not accept. When this pattern was understood, the technical response became one of my simply saying, "Well, what did I do this time?" She would tell me what had made her angry, and her headache would disappear.

Offering and Demonstrating Availability When Such Clearly is Needed

Need is evidenced in the patient's inhibited or overtly anxious transference reaction to interruption of the treatment, whether the interruption is due to a usual or a weekend interval between appointments, or to a longer interval for reasons such as a vacation. The analyst's response may include touching base with the patient by telephone, offering interim telephone contact on the patient's initiative, and offering or scheduling an extra appointment. Such availability emulates appropriate parental availability as observed in the appeal cycle. It provides auxiliary regulation pending improvement in the patient's self-regulatory capability.

As was noted, interruption of the treatment relationship caused intense anxiety and phobic symptomatology in the 34-year-old woman with the travel phobia. Early in the analysis, I told her that I was available by phone during my physical absences. She never called me but said that knowing I was potentially available helped her manage her anxiety.

Analyzing the Patient's Repressed Anger and Aggression

Because repressed anger and aggression represent a destructive potential, their exposure can be strongly resisted. Typically, such exposure begins with the analyst's calling attention to the absence of anger in circumstances where anger would be expected. Exposure usually needs to be gradual and within the patient's regulatory tolerance.

Illustration comes from the case of the precocious 17-year-old girl. In what I came to regard as an indirect appeal, she would avert her gaze and look beyond me or at the floor while also becoming silent. We determined that she looked away from me when she was angry at me for something I said or had failed to say. Although we had defined her problem about expressing anger, I felt that it was not being analyzed.

In a particular session, I was pressing the patient to tell me in more detail about her anger as it had begun to surface in that session. She nicely but very firmly told me that she was doing the best she could and that I should back off. My therapeutic zeal had transgressed her tolerance.

Analyzing the Patient's Defensive Inhibitions Against Receiving and Giving Love

Along with the resolution of unconscious anger, freeing the patient to love and experience being loved is essential to the further development and integration of object and self constancy.

After several years of work, the woman with the travel phobia was enjoying improved relations with her husband and her children. She expressed gratitude to me for my help. I responded that I was pleased to be of help and that I enjoyed working with her. In the next session she reported a highly eroticized, frightening dream. With abandon, she was dancing with a gray-haired man. She noted that there were two gray-haired men in her life, her internist and her analyst. While dancing, the internist whispers in her ear that he has "Ace." The dream abruptly stops and she awakens with the thought that "Ace" is a disguise for "AIDS."

Her associations to the dream expressed elements of oedipal and preoedipal conflict. I interpreted the conflicts on both developmental levels. Because it was more prominent in the transference, I focused on her reaction to expressing gratitude. I said that the "AIDS" dream expressed her fear of being punished for wanting to be lovingly close. She said that she has always had difficulty expressing her loving feelings. She fears being rejected as unworthy of love. She became aware that she tended to use her sexuality, as in the dream, to defend against the hurt of being rejected simply as a person. She felt that the love she received in early childhood was conditional. It was not for her as her unique, individual self but for the child her mother needed and wanted her to be.

Conclusion

I have endeavored to convey the contribution of separation-individuation theory to the psychoanalytic understanding of development and pathogenesis, the contribution of the inter-actional, developmental model of the psychoanalytic relationship to psychoanalytic technique, and the process of structural change as it involves the undoing of pathology and the resumption of development.

ACKNOWLEDGMENTS

It is with gratitude that I acknowledge the contribution to this chapter of the members of the Study Group on Adult Development at the San Francisco Psychoanalytic Institute: John Curtis, Ph.D., Milton Lozoff, M.D., George Silberschatz, Ph.D., Earl J. Simburg, M.D.

REFERENCES

Alexander, F., and French, T. M. (1946). The principle of flexibility. In *Psychoanalytic Therapy: Principles and Application*. New York: Ronald.

Emde, R. N. (1980). Ways of thinking about new knowledge and further research from a developmental orientation. *Psychoanalytic and Contemporary Thought* 3:213–235.

Erikson, E. H. (1950). *Childhood and Society*. New York: W. W. Norton.

Freud, S. (1905). Three essays on the theory of sexuality. *Standard Edition* 7:135–243. London: Hogarth.

_____ (1923). The ego and the id. *Standard Edition* 19:13–66. London: Hogarth.

_____ (1930). Civilization and its discontents. *Standard Edition* 21:59–145. London: Hogarth.

_____ (1940). An outline of psychoanalysis. *Standard Edition* 23:141–207. London: Hogarth.

Hartmann, H. (1952). Mutual influences in the development of the ego and the id. *Psychoanalytic Study of the Child* 7:9–30. New York: International Universities Press.

Loewald, H. W. (1960). On the therapeutic action of psycho-analysis. *International Journal of Psycho-Analysis* 41:16–33.

_____ (1970). Psychoanalytic theory and psychoanalytic process. *Psychoanalytic Study of the Child* 25:45–68. New York: International Universities Press.

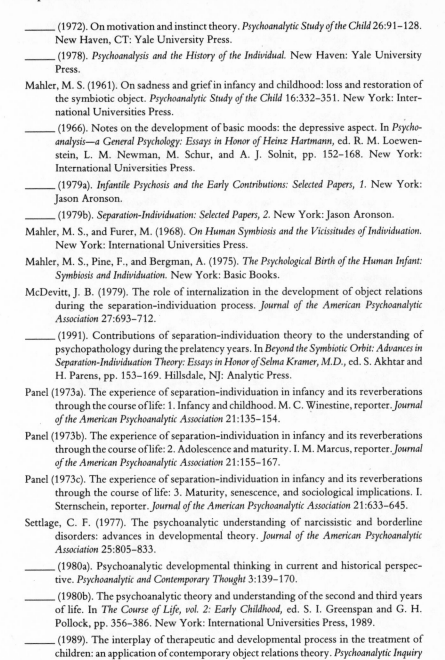
———— (1972). On motivation and instinct theory. *Psychoanalytic Study of the Child* 26:91–128. New Haven, CT: Yale University Press.

———— (1978). *Psychoanalysis and the History of the Individual.* New Haven: Yale University Press.

Mahler, M. S. (1961). On sadness and grief in infancy and childhood: loss and restoration of the symbiotic object. *Psychoanalytic Study of the Child* 16:332–351. New York: International Universities Press.

———— (1966). Notes on the development of basic moods: the depressive aspect. In *Psychoanalysis—a General Psychology: Essays in Honor of Heinz Hartmann,* ed. R. M. Loewenstein, L. M. Newman, M. Schur, and A. J. Solnit, pp. 152–168. New York: International Universities Press.

———— (1979a). *Infantile Psychosis and the Early Contributions: Selected Papers, 1.* New York: Jason Aronson.

———— (1979b). *Separation-Individuation: Selected Papers, 2.* New York: Jason Aronson.

Mahler, M. S., and Furer, M. (1968). *On Human Symbiosis and the Vicissitudes of Individuation.* New York: International Universities Press.

Mahler, M. S., Pine, F., and Bergman, A. (1975). *The Psychological Birth of the Human Infant: Symbiosis and Individuation.* New York: Basic Books.

McDevitt, J. B. (1979). The role of internalization in the development of object relations during the separation-individuation process. *Journal of the American Psychoanalytic Association* 27:693–712.

———— (1991). Contributions of separation-individuation theory to the understanding of psychopathology during the prelatency years. In *Beyond the Symbiotic Orbit: Advances in Separation-Individuation Theory: Essays in Honor of Selma Kramer, M.D.,* ed. S. Akhtar and H. Parens, pp. 153–169. Hillsdale, NJ: Analytic Press.

Panel (1973a). The experience of separation-individuation in infancy and its reverberations through the course of life: 1. Infancy and childhood. M. C. Winestine, reporter. *Journal of the American Psychoanalytic Association* 21:135–154.

Panel (1973b). The experience of separation-individuation in infancy and its reverberations through the course of life: 2. Adolescence and maturity. I. M. Marcus, reporter. *Journal of the American Psychoanalytic Association* 21:155–167.

Panel (1973c). The experience of separation-individuation in infancy and its reverberations through the course of life: 3. Maturity, senescence, and sociological implications. I. Sternschein, reporter. *Journal of the American Psychoanalytic Association* 21:633–645.

Settlage, C. F. (1977). The psychoanalytic understanding of narcissistic and borderline disorders: advances in developmental theory. *Journal of the American Psychoanalytic Association* 25:805–833.

———— (1980a). Psychoanalytic developmental thinking in current and historical perspective. *Psychoanalytic and Contemporary Thought* 3:139–170.

———— (1980b). The psychoanalytic theory and understanding of the second and third years of life. In *The Course of Life, vol. 2: Early Childhood,* ed. S. I. Greenspan and G. H. Pollock, pp. 356–386. New York: International Universities Press, 1989.

———— (1989). The interplay of therapeutic and developmental process in the treatment of children: an application of contemporary object relations theory. *Psychoanalytic Inquiry* 9:375–396.

_____ (1990). Childhood to adulthood: structural change in development toward independence and autonomy. In *New Dimensions in Adult Development,* ed. R. A. Nemiroff and C. A. Colarusso, pp. 26–43. New York: Basic Books.

_____ (1991). On the treatment of preoedipal pathology. In *Beyond the Symbiotic Orbit: Advances in Separation-Individuation Theory: Essays in Honor of Selma Kramer, M.D.,* ed. S. Akhtar and H. Parens, pp. 351–367. Hillsdale, NJ: Analytic Press.

_____ (1992). Psychoanalytic observations on adult development in life and in the therapeutic relationship. *Psychoanalytic and Contemporary Thought* 15:349–374.

_____ (1993). Therapeutic process and developmental process in the restructuring of object and self constancy. *Journal of the American Psychoanalytic Association* 41:473–492.

Settlage, C. F., Bemesderfer, S., Rosenthal, J., et al. (1991). The appeal cycle in early mother–child interaction: the nature and implications of a finding from developmental research. *Journal of the American Psychoanalytic Association* 39:987–1014.

Settlage, C. F., Curtis, J., Lozoff, M., et al. (1988). Conceptualizing adult development. *Journal of the American Psychoanalytic Association* 36:347–369.

Settlage, C. F., Rosenthal, J., Spielman, P. M., et al. (1990). An exploratory study of mother–child interaction during the second year of life. *Journal of the American Psychoanalytic Association* 38:705–731.

Settlage, C. F., Silver, D. H., Afterman, J., et al. (1993). Developmental process: mother–child and father–child interaction during the second year of life. In *Family, Self, and Society: Toward a New Agenda for Family Research,* ed. P. A. Cowan, D. Field, D. Hansen, et al., pp. 363–384. Hillsdale, NJ: Lawrence Erlbaum Associates.

Stern, D. N. (1985). *The Interpersonal World of the Infant: A View from Psychoanalysis and Developmental Psychology.* New York: Basic Books.

Stone, L. (1961). *The Psychoanalytic Situation: An Examination of Its Development and Essential Nature.* New York: International Universities Press.

3

Application of the Appeal Cycle to the Psychoanalysis of Adults

Discussion of Settlage's Chapter "On the Contribution of Separation-Individuation Theory to Psychoanalysis: Developmental Process, Pathogenesis, Therapeutic Process, and Technique"

Mary Anne Delaney, M.D.

As the process of reforging the health care system continues in the United States, the field of mental health has begun to focus more intensely on the question of the efficacy of psychotherapy and psychoanalysis. Not only is determining the overall efficacy of these treatments an important area of research and evaluation, but also those factors operating in the treatment situation that contribute to efficacy are worthy of examination. In prior psychotherapeutic research studies, one of the critical elements of effective interactions between the psychotherapist and the patient that has been identified is the psychotherapist's capacity to convey to the patient that the therapist has empathy for the patient's concerns, conflicts, and feelings. Although from different perspectives, both Kohut and Mahler have focused on the role of empathy in the psychoanalytic situation. Kohut has examined directly the curative action of the psychoanalyst's empathic response to the patient. Mahler has emphasized the critical importance of the mother's empathic response to the child in

55

enabling the child to develop throughout the separation-individuation process in appropriate ways. Settlage, drawing on Mahler's observations, further contributes to our understanding of the role of empathy in the developmental process and in the pathogenesis of conflictual difficulties, and goes on to examine how developmental difficulties are expressed in the psychoanalytic treatment situation.

SETTLAGE'S DEVELOPMENTAL OBSERVATIONS

Settlage grounds his work in separation-individuation theory. While the entire process of achieving autonomy is based on interactions, in the rapprochement subphase the interaction between the mother and child is crucial. When the child expresses impulses and feelings, the mother acknowledges, labels, responds to, and regulates those impulses and feelings in the interactional sphere between the mother and child. This results in the child developing much-needed identifications, age-appropriate ego functions, and superego capacities that will enable the child to use and develop adaptive defense mechanisms in situations where loss and anxiety arise.

In interactions between the parent and the child that are less than optimal and may result in pathogenic adaptation, the parent may respond to the child's impulses and feelings in any of several ways. It is essential for the child to experience from the parent encouragement and sanctioning of the child's efforts to separate and individuate. Failure to support the child in these efforts leads the child to mistrust his or her impulses to become a separate and distinct individual. Also, as the child begins to separate and individuate, any anger he or she experiences due to the loss of closeness to the mother must be acknowledged by the mother. The mother must attempt to reestablish the relationship in order to assist the child in modulating the anger. If the mother fails to assuage the child's anger at the loss and reestablish the relationship, the child's capacity to regulate the experience of anger can be compromised. Finally, the mother who has an excessive need to control the child in his or her attempts either to express feelings of anger or anxiety or to explore the environment and return to the mother will not only hamper the child's autonomy but also preclude the child from developing the capacity to respond to and regulate his or her feelings.

Thus, it can be surmised that the mother who is best able to contribute positively to her child's resolution of the rapprochement subphase is the mother who has the capacity to empathize. Such mothers are capable of affectively reading their child's impulses and feelings and responding to them productively rather than simply reacting on the basis of the mother's own inherent conflicts.

In the interaction between the child and the mother during the rapprochement subphase, the child's response is to develop defensive operations that enable the child to cope with the individuation process and the mother's interaction patterns. Settlage identifies several defensive constellations that the child may use, for example, too close identification with the mother, identification with the aggressor, omnipotent defenses and behaviors, and precocious development. All of these defensive constellations represent attempts by the immature ego to handle the wishes and feelings that the mother has not been able to assist the child in regulating in the mother–child interaction. The child's responses, particularly those of anger and aggression toward the mother who cannot assist the child in reestablishing the relationship with her, can lead to an injured sense of self and an underlying self-perception incorporated by the child that he or she is bad and that his or her urges and feelings are unacceptable.

Settlage hypothesizes that in the analytic treatment situation, especially during separations of the patient from the analyst, the same issues reemerge. It is incumbent upon the analyst to recognize that the analyst's and patient's reactions to separations are often reenactments of the failure of the mother–child interaction that the patient experienced during the separation-individuation process. In the course of the analysis it is critical that the same anger and aggression that the patient exhibited as a toddler needs to be revealed in the analytic process with the analyst serving to assist the patient in the regulation of the experience of this affect and the expression of the affect. With the uncovering of the anger that had heretofore been unconscious and the analysis of the defensive maneuvers that the patient used to maintain the unconscious nature of this anger, the patient becomes free to experience loving and being loved.

Settlage's observations about the separation-individuation process and its applications to clinical psychoanalytic theory arise from his analytic work and from direct observation of mothers and children. To further his observational work Settlage and his colleagues have devised an observational technique known as the Semistructured Observation Situation (SSOS) (Settlage et al. 1990). In this research situation, the child–parent interaction is observed while the mother gradually turns her attention away from the child first by answering the telephone, then by interacting with an interviewer, and, finally, by leaving the room. The mother and child are then reunited after 3 to 5 minutes.

During this observation, the mother's response to the child is rated for the mother's capacity for empathy, maintaining attentiveness to the child when her attention becomes divided, setting limits, and respecting the child's autonomous strivings. An overall score of the effectiveness of the parent–child interaction is also assigned.

Concurrent with the SSOS, the child's functioning is also observed in the Play Group Observational Situation (PGOS). During the PGOS, index children interacted with other children and have access to their mothers, though often from another room. A child's behavior is rated for curiosity, exploration, play, coping, social relations, maintaining a relationship with the mother, modulation of aggression, and interacting with the environment. An overall functioning rating for the child is also made by the researchers.

In the course of conducting these observations, Settlage has identified a mother–child interactional pattern that he calls the "appeal cycle." In this cycle, the child responds to the mother's lessened attention with increasing distress. The child then "appeals" to the mother either directly or indirectly through behaviors that cannot be ignored. If the mother senses and responds appropriately to the child's distress, the child can return to his or her previous level of adaptive, independent functioning.

The observational situations described by Settlage et al. (1990) are similar to that used by Ainsworth et al. (1978) to assess children's responses to separation from their mothers in unfamiliar situations. The Strange Situation (SS), while differing from the SSOS in some respects, has been frequently replicated and widely researched. The Strange Situation is based primarily on the actual physical absence of the mother who leaves the room while the child remains with a stranger. The SSOS does eventuate with the mother leaving the room but only after gradually turning her attention from the child.

Some of the criticisms of the Ainsworth Strange Situation may also be applied to the SSOS. It is difficult in any cross-sectional study to establish the predictive value of the single observation. Matas and colleagues (1978) have correlated ratings during the Strange Situation with play capacities and social competence at later ages. However, some have argued that a child's temperament, especially a tendency to distress in new situations, may be a stronger element operating in the Strange Situation than the quality of the child's attachment to the mother (Kagan 1984). Thus, temperament, as a very basic quality that a child brings to any situation, may be accounting for any predictive ability. Settlage's SSOS has the advantage of being rated along with the PGOS and thus is not as narrowly focused as the Strange Situation. However, the question of predictive value remains without sufficient follow-up studies. Additionally, if one intends, as does Settlage, to apply the appeal cycle paradigm to adult functioning, answering the question of how well these observations relate to other aspects of a child's current and future functioning, let alone to adult functioning, is critical.

One particular question that arises in interpreting the findings from the SSOS and the PGOS, in addition to the contribution of overall temperament to the child's response to these situations, is the contribution of the strength of the aggressive drive in an individual child in determing the child's behavior. It could be postulated that children endowed with more robust aggressive drives might be more easily overwhelmed as they experienced greater anger as the mother progressively withdraws from them. Whatever the mother's empathic response and soothing behaviors were, such children might not reorganize as quickly and adaptively as some other children. The interplay between each child and mother is profoundly affected by that child's temperament and drive endowment and must be considered, heavily, in interpreting the results of both the Strange Situation and the SSOS.

The Strange Situation was originally developed and used with American children. Settlage's sample for the SSOS were Caucasian Americans. When the Strange Situation has been used with children of other cultures, for example, Japanese children (Bretherton and Waters 1985), different results have been obtained. Japanese children generally react with considerable distress to their mothers leaving the room. Rather than immediately characterizing these children as "insecurely attached," the fact that Japanese children are rarely separated from their mothers needs to be taken into account. The same cautions about generalizing the findings of the types of attachment seen in the Strange Situation to all cultures would seem to apply to generalizing the findings of the SSOS to children of other cultures and, by extension, to adults reared in other cultural environments.

In addition to temperament, drive endowment, and cultural influences, another factor affecting a child's response to the mother's libidinal or actual separation may be gender. While findings of significant statistical differences between boys and girls in the expression of feelings of distress are rare, there does seem to be some indication that boys may show more distress in new or strange situations when compared with girls (Smith 1974). When boys and girls reach school age, this difference disappears. Awareness of these possible gender differences is important in interpreting the findings of both the Strange Situation and the SSOS. Girls may develop emotional control more quickly than boys and may appear less distressed about separations. Whether girls are, in fact, less distressed is more difficult to measure and may be harder for mothers to read as well.

Both the Strange Situation and the SSOS, despite the drawbacks inherent in both, have emphasized the critical importance of the mother–child interaction in developing attachment styles and adaptive and satisfying object relationships. While both contributions are crucial, caution should be exercised in reaching the conclusion from these studies that the mother is responsible for failures of attachment and object relationships as well as successes in coping with loss in childhood or adulthood. Aside from the child's contributions to the success or failure of their own development, the role of the father and other caregivers needs to be examined. For example, a father's capacity to empathize with a child's distress and tolerate a child's expression of this distress seems enormously critical to a child's developing a healthy self-concept. In addition, fathers also provide their children with important modeling of adaptive coping with loss and fearful circumstances. Fathers who have difficulties with empathizing with their children, responding appropriately to their children, and coping with their own anger and anxiety may have as much impact on their children as do the mothers.

Thus, it is apparent that interpretation of the findings of the Strange Situation and the SSOS is difficult. Each child brings to these situations a complex mixture of resources, liabilities, and experiences that are difficult to capture during a brief moment in time. Likewise, parenting is far too complex a phenomenon to be truly understood in the context of a single interaction with a child. What emerges from both these research studies and seems significant, however, is the importance of the interplay between the parent and the child in modulating the child's response to libidinal and/or actual loss.

TECHNICAL IMPLICATIONS

Recognizing the importance of this interaction in the development of the infant and toddler, Settlage postulates that the analytic situation presents a similar opportunity in adult life for interaction to facilitate development. Settlage suggests that the analyst is analogous to the parent in empathizing with and appropriately responding to a patient's attempts to deal with the loss of the analyst either during inevitable breaks in the analysis or after termination. As the patient recognizes, through analytic work, his or her anger and anxiety about loss and develops more adaptive defenses to handle these affects, the patient is able to resume the process of becoming independent, which had gone awry during his or her early development.

Settlage's emphasis on the need for the analyst, like the "good" parent, to be able to empathize with a patient's distress, whatever it may be, seems pivotal. Unless the analyst, very much like the parent, can see beyond the patient's defensive maneuvers to the conflict underneath, the patient will never be free to develop further. Likewise if the analyst, like the parent, has barriers to paying sufficient "attention" to the patient, the patient's distress and its causes may never be clear to the analyst or the patient.

Settlage stresses the interactional aspects of the analytic situation as well as the critical role of the analyst's empathy. He notes that maintaining anonymity about the analyst's personal life is not the same as concealing the analyst's humanity. Such occurrences as the analyst's obvious emotional response to material about loss can assist the patient in engaging in the analytic process. These types of interactions not only facilitate engagement but also promote a patient's acceptance and tolerance of distressing affective states.

Other aspects of the application to the clinical situation of the phenomenon of the appeal cycle, such as being appropriately available to patients by telephone, are developed throughout Settlage's paper. The techniques suggested are aimed at enabling the patient to resume normal developmental processes that had gone awry secondary to inappropriate or inadequate child–parent interactions during the patient's early years.

The difficulties inherent in drawing conclusions from observing young children in the SSOS are considerable. There are, likewise, conceptual problems inherent in applying a finding from child observation, that is, the appeal cycle, to the adult analytic situation. While Settlage clearly often notes that the observational and the analytic situation are merely analogous and not exactly similar, it is of great importance to maintain the distinction between the two. For example, infants and toddlers actually need their parents to provide ego supports for them during times of distress. Adults, even those with ego difficulties, do not, even though they may yearn for such soothing. Such differences between adults and children are numerous and critical. Settlage is aware of these differences in his conceptualization of the developmental aspects of the psychoanalytic process. Anyone applying Settlage's techniques should maintain these distinctions just as exquisitely.

CONCLUSION

In summary, despite the limitations of the findings from the direct observation of mothers and their children during the Semistructured Observational Situation, the SSOS has allowed Settlage and his colleagues to identify an important interaction between mothers and children during the rapprochement subphase. This interaction, the appeal cycle, illustrates the critical role of maternal empathy in child development. Recognizing this and other elements of the appeal cycle in the psychoanalysis of adults allows patients to achieve greater autonomy and capacities to love and be loved.

REFERENCES

Ainsworth, M. D. S., Blehar, M. C., Waters, W., and Wall, S. (1978). *Patterns of Attachment: A Psychological Study of the Strange Situation*. Hillsdale, NJ: Lawrence Erlbaum.

Bretherton, I., and Waters, E., eds. (1985). Growing points of attachment theory and research. Monographs of the Society for Research in Child Development 50:1–2. Abstract, p. vi. Chicago: University of Chicago Press.

Kagan, J. (1984). *The Nature of the Child*. New York: Basic Books.

Matas, L., Arend, R., and Sroufe, L. (1978). The continuity of adaptation in the second year: the relationship between quality of attachment and later competence. *Child Development* 49:547–556.

Settlage, C. F., Rosenthal, J., Spielman, P. M., et al. (1990). An exploratory study of mother–child interaction during the second year of life. *Journal of the American Psychoanalytic Association* 38:705–731.

Smith, P. K. (1974). Social and situational determinants of fear in the playgroup. In *The Origins of Fear*, ed. M. Lewis, and L. A. Rosenblum, pp. 107–129. New York and London: Wiley.

4

Selfobject Experiences: Development, Psychopathology, Treatment

Ernest S. Wolf, M.D.

This chapter provides an overview of psychoanalytic self psychology as it has been developed by Heinz Kohut and his colleagues. In accordance with the theme of this book, I will highlight the development of the self, its psychopathology, and the treatment of disorders of the self.

Self psychology is not a monolithic theory. Various self psychology researchers, including Kohut himself, explored in different directions guided by their own preferences. Contradictory conclusions sometimes result. Nevertheless, there is a core of self psychology theories and practices that is generally accepted by most workers in the field, although the views presented here reflect especially the particular directions of my own interests, experiences, and conceptualizations.

BASIC ASSUMPTIONS

Psychoanalysis investigates the domain of inner experiences. The neonate is born preadapted to an average expectable environment. Physiologically that means being born with a predictable need for a certain level of oxygen, for nourishment, for warmth, for a certain amount of physical activity, and for protection against physical trauma. Analogously the neonate arrives with a predictable need for psychological experiences, especially for an attuned responsiveness from the caregivers. There also appears to be a universal need to explore the surround, both sensorically and motorically, leading to interactions with the human as well as the nonhuman environment. Comparable to the intake and output of physiological metabolism, one can hypothesize a psychological give-and-take interaction that is needed for psychological growth and development.[1] Self psychology has brought to the study of these phenomena an emphasis on the infant's subjective experience.

SUBJECTIVITY AND SELFOBJECT EXPERIENCES

Fueled by the inborn need to explore and have experiences, the neonate's sensory organs feed a plethora of sensations into the central nervous system. Basch (1975) demonstrated that ordering is the basic function of the brain. Apparently it is a property of the nervous systems of living organisms to organize the sensory experiences into patterns. To the organism these patterns yield information to guide interaction with the surround. Analogously to brain functioning, ordering is also the central organizing principle of psychological functioning (Terman 1992). In the human these patterns and organizations of experiences become very complex. From the point of view

1. Lichtenberg (1989) has presented a comprehensive discussion of the various development factors from the point of view of motivation.

of subjective experience this ordering manifests as attempts to make sense of one's experiences, that is, to confer meaning. For example, the medical student who for the first time peers into a microscope sees only a chaos of confusing dots, lines, and curves without apparent structure; later, after months of immersion into the experience of microscopy, that same student will see cells and nuclei, boundaries and spaces. Analogously, the budding psychotherapist when first confronted with a suffering client or patient, will only hear and see the surface manifestations of psychic pain and pleasure. A few months, or, perhaps, a few years later, after much immersion into the inner life of self and others, this therapist will recognize patterns of the client's deep inner experiences; she has learned to organize her perceptions, that is, she has learned to become empathic with her patient.

Of the numerous patterns of experiences that the infant begins to organize we are particularly interested in those that give the developing youngster a sense of self. Those experiences that become organized to evoke a sense of self we have designated as *selfobject experiences*.[2]

The selfobject concept arose from Kohut's repeated clinical observation that patients' smooth functioning as well as their feeling of well-being were lost when these patients experienced the analyst as not being empathically in tune. He theorized that the self, in order to emerge from a less differentiated matrix, needs certain kinds of inputs from objects to achieve and maintain the self's cohesion, boundaries, vitality,

2. In the recent history of the development of psychoanalytic thinking one can detect a shift of emphasis from a natural science positivist-objectivism to a more experience-near subjective point of view. In harmony with this tendency one can observe a shift from Kohut's emphasis on selfobjects as objects or persons used by the subject in the service of the subject's self [cf. Lichtenberg (1991)] to contemporary emphasis on the subjective aspects of the experience of self and its selfobjects.

and balance. In the psychoanalytic clinical situation the analyst's empathic understanding of the patient may be experienced by the patient as a needed input to evoke and maintain the structural cohesion and energic vitality of the self. Since this needed input for the self is supplied by objects, Kohut termed these objects *selfobjects*. Precisely defined, a selfobject is neither self nor object, but the subjective aspect of a self-sustaining function performed by a relationship of self to objects, who by their presence or activity evoke and maintain the self and the experience of selfhood. As such, the selfobject relationship refers to an intrapsychic experience and does not describe the interpersonal relationship between the self and other objects.

Thus the major forces motivating behavior were seen to emerge as a consequence of the infant's development within a matrix of *selfobject relationships*. In interaction with biological givens and environmental variables, these early relationships are the primary shapers of the personality and account for much adult behavior, whether normal or pathological. Self psychology, therefore, is characterized by a shift in emphasis away from ascribing major motivational force to instinctual drives and, instead, the interactional context is stressed as the major *fons et origo* from which are derived the shape of the self and the impact of its vicissitudes. The self psychological emphasis on the experience of relationships occurred against a background of similar findings emerging from infant research. Current self psychological theorizing seeks to integrate the data from clinical psychoanalysis with the data from infant research. Developmental research demonstrates increasing recognition of the importance of mutual regulation between caregiver and child. Analogous paradigm shifts with their emphasis on interactional dynamics can be seen in Kohut's self psychological theorizing, in Mitchell's relational theories, in Lichtenberg's motivational systems, and in Stolorow's intersubjectivity theory as well as in the recent work of Gill and Hoffman.

SELFOBJECT EXPERIENCES

Selfobject experiences are needed for the emergence and maintenance of a cohesive, balanced, and energetic self. These selfobject experiences can be classified into various types: mirroring, idealizing, alter ego, ally–antagonist, efficacy, vitalization of affects, and perhaps others not yet discovered.

> Throughout his life a person will *experience* himself as a cohesive harmonious firm unit in time and space, connected with his past and pointing meaningfully into a creative-productive future, [but] only as long as, at each stage in his life, he experiences certain representatives of his *human* surroundings as joyfully responding to him, as available to him as sources of idealized strength and calmness, as being silently present but in essence like him, and, at any rate, able to grasp his inner life more or less accurately so that their responses are attuned to his needs and allow him to grasp their inner life when his is in need of assistance. [Kohut 1984, p. 52; italics added]

An optimal *developmental ambience* will provide the child with the essential selfobject experiences. A faulty developmental ambience results in selfs that are impaired in structure and functioning. Such a pathogenic developmental ambience usually is characterized by absent or by noxious selfobject experiences. Faulty selfobject experiences may occur because of unavailability of suitable others through, for example, separation, loss, unresponsiveness, excessive responsiveness, rejection, intrusion, instability, overstimulation, understimulation, inappropriate sexual stimulation, and destructive aggression.

SELFOBJECT EXPERIENCES AND
SELFOBJECT TRANSFERENCES

We have often used the term *fragmentation*, perhaps somewhat too loosely, to characterize the rainbow of self states from the slightest disconcertedness to massively irreversible psychotic disorganization associated with possible loss of self. The intensity of selfobject experiences ranges widely from a fleeting hurt to the deep pain, including anxiety and depression, that is characteristic of disrupted intimate relationships to significant others such as parents, spouses, children, friends, and lovers. And, of course, in a normally proceeding analysis the relationship to one's analyst usually deepens and intensifies while manifesting the characteristic expectations and fears of this particular individual's yearnings for selfobject experiences. In this latter instance we refer to them as *selfobject transferences* since, typically, they are an expression of current needs shaped by the expectations molded in the furnace of early experiences with parents and significant others.

The need for selfobject experiences is not restricted to early development but remains throughout life. The self is enhanced and strengthened by being appropriately responded to. "But this increased firmness does not make the self independent of selfobjects. Instead, it increases the self's ability to use selfobjects for its own sustenance, including an increased freedom in choosing selfobjects" (Kohut 1984, p. 77).

Needed Selfobject Experiences

Kohut originally described three kinds of selfobject relationships. We now recognize at least seven types of selfobject experiences that are needed for the establishment and maintenance of a cohesive, energetic, and balanced self:

1. *Mirroring selfobject experiences*: a need to feel recognized and affirmed; to feel accepted, appreciated, and responded to.

2. *Idealizing selfobject experiences*: a need to experience oneself as being part of an admired and respected selfobject other; a need for the opportunity to be accepted by, and merge into, a stable, calm, nonanxious, powerful, wise, protective other who possesses qualities the subject experiences as lacking in the self.

3. *Merger selfobject experiences*: a primitive form of the mirroring need that finds confirmation of self only in the experience of being totally one with the selfobject. The expansion of the infant's self-experience beyond the boundaries of its body to include aspects of the surround has sometimes been termed infantile grandiosity, which is misleading because the infant is grandiose only in the eyes of the external observer. For the infant it is a real experience of blissful well-being that forms the bedrock upon which healthy self-esteem is built.

4. *Alter-ego selfobject experiences*: a need to experience an essential alikeness with the selfobject. This forms the basis for many important peer relationships that, via imitation, lead to learning. Faced with growing up in a world experienced as alien, the child sometimes manifests the intensity of this need in the creation of imaginary playmates. Might this be a precursor to later artistic creativity?

5. *Adversarial selfobject experiences*: a need to experience the selfobject as a benignly opposing other who continues to be supportive and responsive while allowing or even encouraging the self to be in active opposition and thus confirming an at least partial autonomy; the need for the availability of a selfobject experience of assertive and adversarial confrontation vis-à-vis the selfobject without the loss of self-sustaining responsiveness from that selfobject (cf., e.g., the "no, no, no" of the 2-year-old).

6. *Efficacy experiences*: From the awareness of having an initiating and causal role in bringing about states of needed responsiveness from others, the infant acquires an experience

of efficacy that becomes an essential aspect of the cohesive self experience. It is as if the infant were able to say: I can elicit a response, therefore I am somebody. The regression facilitated during the analysis of adults opens the way to reexperiencing on an archaic level the pleasurable self-enhancing experience of efficacy and the painful self-destroying experience of the loss of efficacy.[3]

7. *Vitalizing selfobject experiences*: The child needs to have the vitalizing experience that the caregiver is affectively attuned to the dynamic shifts or patterned changes in its inner state, that is, across the specific categories of affect to the crescendos and decrescendos, to the surges and fades of the intensity, timing, and shape of its experiences (Stern 1985).

PHASES OF DEVELOPMENT

The developmental line of selfobject relations represents one way to conceptualize the changing requirements for selfobject experiences (Wolf 1980). Kohut (1984) pointed out that "we

---

3. The sense of agency implied in the ability to elicit a response from selfobject-others is one of the strongest supports of the self as a structure and self-esteem as an experience. When the caregiver, usually the mother, out of an excessive zeal to respond, gratifies the child's every need immediately, perhaps even before the child itself has become quite aware of the need, then the experience of having a need and eliciting a response is interfered with. Often such children cannot even fully experience their own affects because they are drowned out by the caregiver's excessively sympathetic response. For example, the child falls, hurts a little, and cries but the child does not feel its pain when the caregiver is overinvolved and cries out loudly in more pain than the child. No joy or pleasure, no pain or sorrow is not immediately taken over and experienced by the caregiver. The child begins to experience itself as an extension of the selfobject-other rather than as a self in its own right, and in the absence of being effective selfs such children lack all sense of efficacy. Thus arises the need to be effective as one's own self by doing something that the caregiver could not possibly resonate with and participate in. I have seen cases of anorexia nervosa where the need to starve oneself was the expression of the underlying need to be effective in the face of an overindulgent and excessively responsive mother.

need investigations of the special selfobject needs of adolescents and the elderly, for example, along with investigations of the selfobject needs that accompany specific life tasks including those shifts to a new cultural milieu that deprive a person of his 'cultural selfobjects,' during his mature years or when he has to deal with a debilitating illness, or the confrontation with death" (p. 194).

The Emergence of the Self

Chronologically, we see first the *preemergent phase*, that is, the developmental phase *before* the first initial but transient appearance of the self. Kohut thought this first self emerged around age 18 months. Evidence from infant research and more extensive clinical experience suggests that the self may first emerge much sooner, perhaps even shortly after birth (Stern, 1985). We see, second, the *consolidation phase*, that is, the phase *during* the development from the first initial transient emergence of the self until the definitive consolidation into a cohesive, balanced and harmonious self. During this consolidation phase the self oscillates between various fragile editions of a partially disorganized fragmented self and a self of various states of cohesion and balance with a variety of configurations of ambitions and ideals. Kohut thought the final consolidation takes place during the eighth year of life. It is at that time that a person's inner program of ambitions and goals crystallizes to form the joyful awareness of his/her human self, an awareness of being temporal and of seeking fulfillment via an unrolling destiny with a precarious beginning, a flourishing middle, and a retrospective end. Third, we see the *postconsolidation phase*, the developmental phase that begins *after* this definitive consolidation.

Infancy

Neonates and small infants presumably experience themselves before self/object differentiation as if in a limitless

merger with the world. Even after self/object differentiation
and the emergence, at least transiently, of a structured self
with a sense of selfhood, there occur nonpathological oscilla-
tions between states of merger and states of nonmerger. At a
later age such merger states would be indicative of regression
and, possibly, pathology. The infant requires active confirmation by its selfobjects because such mirroring experiences are
needed to evoke the self structure and its concomitant experience of selfhood. At the same time, the infant needs the
availability of idealizable selfobjects to provide *idealizing selfobject experiences* for the evocation and sustenance of self structure. Both types of experiences are needed throughout life to
evoke and sustain the sense of self. The need to experience the
essential likeness of the selfobject and to be strengthened by its
quietly sustaining presence are probably present already during infancy also. Infant research has demonstrated that these
selfobject experiences are interactively participated in and
mutually enhancing to both infant and caregiver.

Oedipal Period

Selfobject experiences of both the mirroring and idealizing
types as well as alter-ego experiences are required during the
oedipal period in order for the developing self to form adequate gender identity and to prevent the kind of distortions in
self structure that leave a disposition for the later outbreak of
psychoneurosis in adulthood. In outline, the requirements are
as follows:

   Boy: nonseductive confirmation of his autonomy and
maleness by the mother together with her acceptance of his
idealizing needs. Nonaggressive acceptance of the son's adversarial and alter-ego needs by the father.
   Girl: nonseductive confirmation of her autonomy and
femaleness by the father together with his acceptance of her

idealizing needs. Nonaggressive acceptance of the daughter's alter-ego and adversarial needs by the mother.

Self psychologists generally think that the child can traverse the oedipal experience without permanent damage if the parental response is benignly appropriate and not neurotically reactive. Such a healthy developmental ambience may not be very common given the sociocultural tensions characteristic of past and present Western societies. Castration anxiety and penis envy, therefore, are not inescapable experiences for the child but conditional upon the individual parental and sociocultural configurations that impact on the child's development of self.

Especially during latency, but also to some extent throughout life, one observes that selfobjects are needed as models to imitate and to provide the experience of likeness. These alter-ego experiences are prominent in the development of skills. They open an avenue for learning from peers and from parents as models.

Prepuberty

During the prepubertal years a gradual expansion of the various modes of selfobject experiences takes place with a shift away from the early caretakers as the provider of the selfobject function toward teachers, friends, and, most importantly, with a substitution of symbolic selfobjects for the selfobject person. The selfobject modes are becoming more diffuse and less personal.

Adolescence and Young Adulthood

The process begun prepubertally becomes more encompassing and deeper during adolescence. Cognitive development leads to a recognition of parental defects with the inevitable outcome of a rapid de-idealization of the early idealized selfobjects, the parents. Since the self cannot flourish in the selfobject vacuum caused by the sudden and rapid de-idealization of parental imagoes but only in relationship to responsive selfobjects, the adolescent turns to the peer group, to the adolescent subculture and its idols, and to the heroes of cultural history for the needed selfobject sustenance of idealizable selfobject experiences. The availability of the peer group to substitute for parents as idealized selfobjects can be crucial for the maintenance of psychological health. The ability to substitute cultural selfobjects for idealization becomes possible with the increasing capacity for symbolization; for example, heroes of history, art, religion, and ideas can be idealized and thus allow for the adolescent's reconstruction of values and integration into the general culture.

Marriage

Spouses are used by each other for a variety of selfobject functions. Intimacy facilitates controlled regression to primitive merger without fear of irreversibly losing the autonomy of the self. Expansion of self boundaries to include the spouse allows participation in the self-sustaining selfobject experience of the other as if it were the self. On the other hand, frustrations and disappointments in the expected and needed selfobject experiences threaten the cohesion of the self and may lead to behaviors that threaten the marriage.

Parenthood

Ideally parents have sufficiently solid and cohesive selfs to respond with sufficient flexibility and fluidity as needed by their offspring. Fluidity of self boundaries also makes it possible to include children as selfobjects or let them separate autonomously, as needed by both children and parents.

Weissman and Cohen (1985) have demonstrated that the parenting alliance is a needed self–selfobject relationship that is vital to the evolving parenthood experience and other adult tasks.

Middle Age

Facilitated by the waning illusion of immortality and precipitated by incidents that force an increasing awareness of the finality of life, middle age becomes a time for self evaluation. The self's reassessment of itself calls for a readjustment of its goals (social, vocational, career, family) to bring them into harmony with the self's "program of action" (Kohut and Wolf 1978, p. 414) that "strives for fulfillment through the realization of its nuclear ambitions and ideals" (Kohut 1975, p. 757). Significant deviation from the latter result in an experience of nonfulfillment that may eventuate in a so-called midlife crisis.

Old Age

Old age is characterized by a reciprocal need to idealize the community and be idealized by it. Old people yearn to be confirmed as an especially valuable guide and model for the community's ideals, which satisfies both their mirroring and efficacy needs. The honors that society often bestows on its aging members testifies to its idealizing needs even though not every council of elders deserves the recognition and power that is entailed.[4]

---

4. The selfobject experiences needed to reach and sustain a maturity of the self include a sense of belonging to a respected, perhaps even idealized, community. Belonging to a subgroup that experiences itself as despised or as treated with contempt by the mainstream culture lowers self-esteem and causes intense feelings of helplessness and rage, as we witness in our inner cities every day. The resulting social turmoil is easily misunderstood and often falsely blamed on the individuals

CENTRAL SUBJECTIVITY:
THE SELFOBJECT EXPERIENCE

In self psychology theory there has been a subtle but discernible shift in our major focus toward the selfobject rather than the self as our center of conceptual gravity. This shift has come about for a number of reasons among which I would point to the inescapable recognition that we never observe selfs in a vacuum, so to speak, but only within a framework of a matrix of selfobject experiences provided by the functioning of selfobjects. The self resists precise definition. The selfobject concept, however, difficult though it is to comprehend at first, can be defined fairly precisely in terms of the self: Selfobject experiences are those experiences that evoke, maintain, and give cohesion to the self. Objects perform many psychological functions for the person; for example, they may give sexual pleasure, they may feed or support in a variety of ways, they may teach skills and protect, and so on. Some of these interpersonal functions that objects perform in a variety of ways may secondarily, because of the pleasure and success they give to the self, be supportive for the self without being necessary for the integrity of the self's structure. These interpersonal functions are to be distinguished from the selfobject functions that as selfobject experiences are sustaining the self.

Let me illustrate this important distinction by recalling,

---

involved or merely on economic conditions. The ethnic violence that is currently so prominent in Europe is perpetrated more by alienated middle-class youth than by economically disadvantaged people. The common denominator is the recent history of social changes that resulted in a fragmentation of societies and led to their inability to continue providing adequate selfobject experiences for its individuals who now experience themselves as weak, helpless, and despised. Through a self-esteem–enhancing process of identification with an historically idealized but aggressively violent aspect of the group, the accumulated narcissistic rage is displaced on others that are even more helpless, for example, by terrorizing powerless foreigners, women, and children, or by such "courageous" acts as the desecration of graves that cannot defend themselves.

for example, a common vicissitude of the student–teacher relationship when, for example, studying music. In the beginning the student uses the teacher to learn some musical skill. It is an interpersonal relationship with an interpersonal function. Often, after a few weeks there may be some disappointments and the relationship can be broken off or the teacher exchanged for another teacher without any psychological pain of any consequence. But sometimes after some months or years, perhaps because of some special need of one of them, but not necessarily an abnormal need, the student–teacher relationship changes; now any disruption is experienced as a significant psychological trauma and may possibly even lead to a psychotic break when one of the two participants breaks off the relationship. One recognizes that an intense reaction has developed, with much emotional turmoil. Some archaic selfobject need has become mobilized and requires a specific selfobject experience in order to maintain the cohesion of the self. Because it manifests in the present as a revival of an archaic need we call this phenomenon a selfobject transference: the self of one or both of the participants has become dependent on the other for the needed selfobject support to its self. What had been an interpersonal relationship dedicated to the acquisition of skills has been superseded by a selfobject experience functioning to maintain the structure and cohesion of the self.

THE UBIQUITY OF THE NEED FOR SELFOBJECT EXPERIENCES

The need for selfobject experiences is not confined to early years but selfobject responses in a variety of forms are needed throughout the life span. Indeed, the need for selfobject responses is always present, waxing and waning with the ups and downs of the strength and vulnerability of the self. At one end of the spectrum, the strong, healthy, and mature self still requires some self-sustaining affirmation even in a nourishingly stimulating environment that is free of noxious stresses; at the other end, the fragile or regressed or otherwise vulnerable self desperately needs the responding experiences exercised by a selfobject matrix to maintain some semblance of self cohesion, even when its fragility has activated powerful defenses, for example, schizoid withdrawal, paranoid hostility, or numbing depression, that frustrate and defeat the very yearning for these selfobject responses.

Similarly, experiences with idealized selfobjects and alter-ego self objects are also needed over a lifetime. As the individual grows and matures from birth to death the original archaic form of the selfobject needs of infancy gradually change into other forms of selfobject needs—sometimes represented symbolically—that are appropriate to the level of maturity reached.

The terminological shift from narcissistic transferences to selfobject transferences has still another significance. While initially Kohut defined the need for mirroring as related to the reactivation of the archaic infantile grandiose self—and this is still true for the early years of childhood and for selfs in a state of relatively deep regression—we can define the need for mirroring now more generally as the universal need of any self to be affirmed as significant. Ideally, perhaps, one can theorize about a self so strong, healthy, and cohesive as to have no need for selfobject experiences of any kind. Clinically, however, one cannot expect to come upon a self that has no selfobject needs, although it may labor under the comforting illusions of independence, autonomy, and self-sufficiency.

PSYCHOPATHOLOGY

Pathogenic selfobject experiences may result in arrested development of a self and/or traumatic injury to a self. Any particular self may show aspects of both types of impairment. If the noxious experience occurred during the preemergent phase of the self, the resulting pathology is likely to be classified as borderline or psychotic. Disturbance of self development during the consolidation phase leads to narcissistic personality and narcissistic behavior disorders. Finally, there are those disturbances that arise from interference by intercurrent events or by the very shortcomings of the self, with the fulfillment of the self's aims as laid down in a program of action at the time of the consolidation of a specific configuration of ambitions and ideals into a cohesive self. In accord with such a classification of developmental phases, one can conceptualize the psychopathological effects originating in these phases, respectively, as those of the deformed self, the fragile self, or the unfulfilled self.

PREEMERGENCE DISORDERS:
THE DEFORMED SELF

Here is an illustrative example of a self whose traumatic and injurious experiences *before* the emergence of a cohesive self became part of the very structure of the self:

> A 50-year-old lawyer, the mother of two boys in college, came into analysis because she felt she could not cope with the demands that her work at the law firm imposed on her. Much of the time she felt irritable and slightly depressed. Her marriage to a successful businessman was becoming strained by their divergent involvements in their own professional fields, without much concern for what the respective spouse was interested in. As a consequence of their divergent interests they became less available to each other as the provider of needed selfobject experiences. Her symptoms increased and she sought treatment.

During the first year of her analysis the husband left Chicago for a business opportunity on the East Coast that required his presence there. She decided to stay and remain in analysis. The geographic separation was soon followed by a divorce. Her irritability became much more severe and it soon became evident that it peaked during weekends. Weekends seemed like "an enormous cavernous space" to her. She said she was not doing anything, like making herself more attractive, because she felt that it makes no difference, no dent, and she will be left alone and abandoned anyway. Her voice did not sound angry but rather pleading, complaining, and suffering. Her feeling helpless and therefore enraged was interpreted as partially evoked by the loss of her husband. In addition it was also recognized that, on weekends, for example, her rage understandably was directed at the analyst for not being available. Similar patterns of helplessness and rage became evident when there were interruptions in the treatment due to vacations.

During the third year of analysis she met, dated, and eventually married a divorced man. Mitch seemed suitable and they appeared to be well attuned to each other, especially since many of his professional interests overlapped with hers. But in spite of this favorable development she did not really lead a more satisfying life. Even though her employers and co-workers respected her for the good job she did, her self-criticism and perception of not really doing a good job or being a good person did not diminish. She acknowledged that the analysis had helped her enough so that she now could do the minimum of work necessary. Nevertheless, she remained always unhappy, on the verge of feeling exhausted, unable to shake off the perception of not being worthwhile, not being able to do anything that would make others look up to her, not being anyone special. A constant feeling of shame and anger at being so ordinary in appearance and in performance pervaded her every day. She could agree that the reality was indeed different but that the feeling, the humiliation, was so strong that it was all that mattered. She recognized that she had always felt this way, since she was a small child of 3 or 4. She connected it to her parents' attitude toward her. Her mother was totally involved in her own unrewarding career as a performing artist and paid little attention to her four children. Her father, an academic in a minor college, was a constant critic of the patient. Moreover, his favorite child was the patient's oldest sister. Thus the patient's experience of herself as a small child convinced her then of her flawed nature and left her with persistent feelings of resentment that isolated her socially from siblings and potential friends.

In this patient the persistence of the symptoms of chronic rage and chronic depressive overlay were relatively independent of any contemporaneous experiences of her selfobject ambience. To be sure there was some exacerbation during the analyst's vacations or on weekends. But generally, whether married or not, whether her husband at the time was understanding or indifferent, regardless of what might be going on in her relationship to her children or to her co-workers, and regardless of the state of the analytic transference, there was only one constant in her life: a chronic unrelenting sense of worthlessness. During the analysis her self-condemnation and depression would increase in response to the analyst's attempts to be empathically attuned. For instance, if the analyst recognized some achievement of the patient she would experience that shamefully as an expectation of future performance that she could not live up to. The disruptions that occurred could sometimes be restored by corrective experiences evoked through interpretations. In general however, the chronic depressive tone was only minimally responsive to analytic interventions and lifted somewhat only gradually after years of analytic treatment.

In this case it seems reasonable to assume that the structure of her self-experience as it was constituted into a cohesive self left her with a distorted view of herself that became part of the very structure of her self. She could remember always having felt bad about her family's emotional poverty, coldness, and rigidity in comparison to the families of schoolmates. Hating herself as part of a family she could neither love nor leave became the essence of her experience of her self. Selfobject experiences per se, especially postconsolidation, were of relatively minor influence in the face of a mainly cohesive but depressed self. An appreciable number of patients that we usually label as borderline fall into this category.

CONSOLIDATION DISORDERS:
THE FRAGILE SELF

A different picture emerges when the trauma to the self is sustained during that part of the self's development that takes place *after* a somewhat cohesive self has initially become established temporarily but *before* the final consolidation of the cohesive, balanced, and vigorous self.

These disturbances arise from injuries that slowed but that did not halt the self's progression to cohesion and vigor. Such a self is left weakened and vulnerable to a repetition of the injurious experience. Defenses are erected to protect against reexperiencing the trauma. These complex structures of vulnerabilities and defenses often burden the individual with great sensitivities that during the analytic process manifest as transference phenomena and that, extra-analytically, make these individuals especially sensitive to the average expectable slights and mild narcissistic injuries of everyday life. It is precisely these experiences of great sensitivity that make an analytic process possible.

A young lawyer, in his third year of analysis, reported that his cat had died. The cat had never been mentioned before and rather perfunctorily, without any real feeling, I acknowledged the loss. A period of silence ensued and I said something like "let's go on." More silence, and I commented that the cat must have been quite important and the loss very painful to the patient. Yes, the cat—he used the cat's name—meant very much to him but he did not think I could understand that. He sounded upset. During the next session he still was upset, as I could tell by his coldly angry voice. I interpreted that he was angry with me for not having been more sympathetic. Yes, he agreed, he did not think I really cared but just like his mother I acted as if I did. Mother would put on a great show of concern, especially when other people were watching, but she didn't really care. I confirmed that I do not feel about pets the same way that he and many other people do but that he must have experienced my comments as pretending concern similar to his mother.

This young man had come into analysis because he was moderately depressed, with much anxiety, but functioning well. His depression was only of short duration and it was significant that life circumstances recently had forced a geographic separation from his family. Though he was in telephone contact and saw his parents several times a year, he now felt alone and without the responsive selfobject ambience that had been a familiar and needed part of his daily life. His exquisite sensitivity to and need for someone to be always intimately attuned to him grew out of some experiences during latency years when other life circumstances also forced a separation from his parents that lasted several months. At that time he was temporarily left in the care of an elderly grandparent. These and other vicissitudes of selfobject experiences could be traced to genetic trauma during the consolidation phase. They were analyzed with great diminishment of the anxiety and depression. Follow-up over several years demonstrated what one might reasonably call a cure of a narcissistic personality disorder.

LIFE CURVE DISORDERS:
THE UNFULFILLED SELF

Finally, there are those disturbances that arise from interference by intercurrent events or by the very shortcomings of the self, with the fulfillment of the self's aims as laid down in a life

curve at the time of the consolidation of a specific configuration of ambitions and ideals into a cohesive self.[5]

> The psychology of the self . . . is time-related par excellence.
> The concept of a nuclear self, of a structure that, once it has
> been established, has, from the beginning, a destiny, a poten-
> tial life curve, and the self-psychological emphasis of the
> relationship in the major disturbances of the self between
> dynamic-structural conceptualizations that are in essence not
> related to the time axis (such as the fragmentation of the self, or
> its weakness, or its lack of harmony), on the one hand, and
> functional failures along the time axis that might lie far away in
> the distant future (such as a lack of fulfillment of creative-
> productive potentialities), on the other hand, differentiate self
> psychological theory in this respect clearly from classical me-
> tapsychology. . . . look at my remarks concerning depressions
> of late middle age (in *The Restoration of the Self*, p. 241) [see next
> paragraph below] as the "pivotal point" in the life curve of the
> self corresponding to the position of the Oedipus complex in
> the classical neuroses). Self psychology recognizes that these
> disturbances are due not to the reactivation of structural ten-
> sions from childhood (such as the ego's reaction to the absence
> of the penis in the girl or the sexual possession of the mother
> by the father) but to the hopelessness of the self to fulfill its
> destiny as laid down in its nuclear ambitions, skills, and ideals.
> [Kohut 1978, p. 594]

While I am thus reluctant to dramatize the establishment of the
self by specifying a definite point at which it is said to be born,
I believe that there is, later in life, a specific point that can be
seen as crucially significant—a point in the life curve of the self
at which a final crucial test determines whether the previous
development had failed or had succeeded. . . . But I am in-

---

5. Goldberg (1990) defines *disorders of continuity* that are related to the life
curve disorders but represent a specific subvariety characterized by disruptions in
the continuity of the self in time and space.

clined to put the pivotal point even later—to late middle age when, nearing the ultimate decline, we ask ourselves whether we have been true to our innermost design. This is the time of utmost hopelessness for some, of utter lethargy, of that depression without guilt and self-directed aggression, which overtakes those who feel that they have failed and cannot remedy the failure in the time and with the energies still at their disposal. [Kohut 1977, p. 241]

The following case will illustrate a disturbance of the self that was associated with a deviation from the life curve of an individual.

This 45-year-old successful options trader came into treatment believing that something was wrong with him because he thought he could not maintain long-term relationships with women. His marriage of over twenty years seemed on the verge of breaking up. He said that he never really felt close to his wife and she complained of his being cold and distant. He wondered whether she might be correct in thinking him unemotional and uninvolved. In spite of these difficulties they generally got along well together, enjoyed a satisfactory sex life, and shared an interest in their two children. Recently, however, he had become intensely infatuated with a woman about twenty years younger than himself whom he had met at an athletic event and he had left the home to be able to spend more time with her. He recognized that aside from the sexual excitement he had no real interest in the young woman who intellectually also was not in his league. The relationship with her lasted only a few months but since then there had been a series of affairs with a number of women from various walks of life. All these involvements were superficial and transient but there was one common denominator in that all of them, in contrast to his wife, shared an interest in camping, horseback riding, bicycling, sailing, scuba diving, athletics—in short, in the physically active outdoors life.

As we gradually reconstructed his history it became clear that his interest in such a physically active life-style had its origin early in his youth and had provided him with a sense of joyous fulfillment. At that time he had felt oppressed and demeaned in his age-appropriate grandiosity by his parent's anxiety. His active life-style of strenuous physical engagement out of doors seemed a reaction to an ambience of excessive caution in the parental home. It restored to him a self-experience of invulnerability by merging with the infinite power and beauty of nature, a particular variety of idealizing selfobject experience, closely related to religious experiences, in which the self merges with the idealized selfobject. During the initial years of his marriage he was forced to restrain these activities because of the demands made on his time by the business he was building up and by the family responsibilities requiring his attention. The achievements attained and the recognition received remained a sufficient source of self-esteem. Eventually the demands by business and family decreased. Now he had both the time and resources to fully engage in the active outdoors life that he had always yearned for. However, being unable to arouse his wife's interest in joining him, he became somewhat depressed and withdrawn unless he was away from home and involved in his various activities.

Another illustrative example:

This young professional woman had been raised in a socially prominent upper-middle-class family whose deep roots in America reached back to prerevolutionary times. Aside from some very early separations from her parents that left her with a tender sensitivity to separation experiences, she developed without major self vulnerabilities. Straight out of college she married appropriately, had children, and became a leader in her social circles. The marriage, however, lacked satisfying personal intimacy, and when the children no longer required her full attendance she embarked on a professional education and career. Here she found some recognition for her abilities and enjoyed the experience of being surrounded by the responsiveness of colleagues and friends. However, the increasing alienation between herself and her husband caused tensions that brought her into analysis. The marriage ended in a divorce that disrupted her social status. She found she was no longer acceptable. An unanticipated social isolation resulted in much anxiety and some depression that could be relieved only temporarily by her professional achievements or by the responsive selfobject ambience created by her colleagues. During the analysis it became quite clear that being an active participant in her social circle leading to an honored position had always been part of her self image as it had been for her mother. Through the analysis she achieved a clarification of her goals that allowed her to make the appropriate changes to bring her unfolding life curve back on track.

THERAPEUTIC CONSIDERATIONS

Pathogenic events lead to a self that is weakened and vulnerable, and, consequently, a self that has developed all kinds of defensive and compensatory functions to safeguard its remaining structures. Therapeutic activity must be directed toward strengthening the self. A strengthened self often is able to give up no longer needed defenses. Interventions aimed directly at defensive structures before strengthening the vulnerable self usually lead to undesirable negative therapeutic reactions. The analyst, therefore, must have a fairly comprehensive grasp of this self's history and development, of the vicissitudes it faced, of the injuries it sustained and of the defensive and compensatory responses it developed to protect and to express itself. Conceptualizing such an understanding requires a theoretical framework that relates data from observations about the patient to the introspective-empathic data experienced by the therapist–patient couple in analytic interaction (Bacal, 1985). There always remain unanswered questions about the relative contribution of genetically determined transferences and defenses versus reactions determined by the here-and-now of the therapeutic encounter. The analysand's unconscious and the analyst's unconscious surely influence each other to an extent that is unknowable by either. A high tolerance of uncertainty as well as a flexible openness to discard what does not work, with a willingness to look again and try something different, characterize the skillful therapist.

Such a therapeutic process rests on what happens between analysand and analyst, especially on the subjective feeling states of each in response to the other. Here I am avoiding the terms *transference* and *countertransference* because they carry the burden of too many contradictory and, therefore, confusing definitions.

Two types of psychotherapy process can be differentiated: the ambient process and the disruption–restoration process.

Ambient Process

This process is indicated for the patient who is in need of selfobject experiences that will nourish arrested and atrophied aspects of an impaired self. The therapist must be sensitive to the empathically perceived inner state of the patient's self and respond appropriately. The patient will feel understood, appreciated, and valued. This provides the patient with a needed selfobject experience that strengthens the patient's self by strengthening the self-selfobject bond between patient and therapist. This process is initiated by providing a nonspecific selfobject ambience that depends as much on the therapist's personality as on the therapist's theoretical orientation. However, this is not to be misunderstood as gratifying or actively soothing the patient except for trying to understand the patient empathically and verbally conveying that understanding. The patient may misperceive such understanding as love, and that can be interpreted.

Disruption–Restoration Process

In a smoothly proceeding psychoanalytic treatment one can observe often, perhaps always, sudden disruptions that transform a relatively harmonious working relationship between analyst and analysand—sometimes referred to as the therapeutic alliance—into an adversarial ambience. It appears that these disruptions occur during all psychoanalytic treatments regardless of the theoretical convictions of the therapist, that is, regardless of whether the analyst thinks of himself as classically or object-relations or self psychologically oriented. However, different theoretical frameworks lead to different conceptualizations of the observed phenomena, indeed, sometimes to entirely different observations altogether. I will attempt to conceptualize within the theoretical framework of psychoanalytic self psychology, but I am aware that the described phenomena could be formulated differently. In a properly conducted psychoanalysis the disruption is followed by a restoration of the collaborative ambience between analysand and analyst. Failing that restoration, the joint psychoanalytic enterprise is likely to founder in a premature termination or in an interminable stalemate (Wolf 1988, 1993).

The disruption is ushered in when the analysand suddenly experiences the analyst as not being attuned or attentive. The patient feels misunderstood and unable to get through to the therapist. Perhaps the therapist seems more interested in himself and in his theories than in the patient's concerns. Or the therapist may seem to be more involved with the patient's family or other presumed adversaries than with the patient. Sometimes the patient has the impression that the analyst is more interested in the patient's behavior than how he or she feels inside or that the analyst cares more about what the analysand does than who he or she is. For the patient it is an experience of ineffectiveness, perhaps sometimes even total powerlessness.

In the past I have on occasion talked about "empathic failure of the therapist" as the cause for the disruption. Let me now correct the erroneous impression that I was blaming the therapist for the disruption. The disruption is not due to a failure of either but due to a discrepancy between the experiences of reality by analysand and by analyst. Analysands unquestionably experience a lack of empathy and understanding. The analyst must recognize and acknowledge that because, by so doing, (1) he provides the patient with an experience of having effectively communicated to the analyst, that is, a self-enhancing experience of efficacy, and (2) he restores the patient's experience of a selfobject bond with the analyst. However, the analyst's acknowledgment of the patient's experience is not a admission of guilt and does not call for an apology. At the most a comment indicating one's understanding of the patient's suffering is in order.

Generally speaking, it is an apparent consequence of such episodes of malattunement that patients feel alone and overwhelmed by affects of anxiety, frustration, anger, helplessness and rage, or hopelessness and depression. It is useful to remember that the disruption of the therapeutic relationship is associated with low self-esteem; that is, a devastating sense of badness characterizes the disrupted state of the analysand. (The self experience of the analyst will qualitatively include some similar feelings if he allows himself to become aware of them, though he may reasonably hope he will be able to resist the regressive and fragmenting pull of the disruption more effectively than the patient can.) These overwhelming affective states are probably related to a resonance with analogous affective reactions during infancy and childhood when the youngster's self-esteem was crushed in interaction with the significant adults.

The acknowledgment by the analyst of his having been

experienced by the analysand in such a way as to trigger the disruption usually leads to a collaborative inquiry by both into the dynamic and genetic causes of the disruption. For the analysand this becomes an experience of being understood, an experience of efficacy in having an influence on the analyst, and, finally, an experience of being vitalized by the affective attunement with the analyst. Due to the intensity of the disruption, the self state is one of a therapeutic regression with a disorganization of various aspects of the self structure. The ties that bind the components of the self together are loosened and subject to rearrangement into a more cohesive configuration in harmony with the relationship with the analyst. As a result the analysand's self is strengthened and the disruption gradually changes into a restoration of an ambience of lowered tension with renewed analytic inquiry. The analysand's self-esteem is enhanced concomitant with the strengthening of the self. This is in contrast with the archaic experience with the selfobjects of childhood. At that time confrontations between child and parent left the child feeling inadequate, bad, and unacceptable, and the child's self was weakened. Now this is partially reversed in the analytic situation. The patient is still the same person with the same self, albeit a little stronger. But what a difference that extra strength makes!

REFERENCES

Bacal, H. (1985). Optimal responsiveness and the therapeutic process. In *Progress in Self Psychology*, vol. 1, ed. A. Goldberg, pp. 220–227. New York: Guilford.

Basch, M. (1975). Toward a theory that encompasses depression: a revision of existing causal hypotheses in psychoanalysis. In: *Depression and Human Existence*, ed. E. J. Anthony and T. Benedek. Boston: Little, Brown.

Gill, M., and Hoffman, I. (1982). *Analysis of Transference*, vol. II. New York: International Universities Press.

Goldberg, A. (1990). *The Prisonhouse of Psychoanalysis*. Hillsdale, NJ: Analytic Press.

Kohut, H. (1975). Remarks about the formation of the self. In *The Search for the Self*, vol. 2, ed. P. Ornstein, pp. 737–770. New York: International Universities Press.

_____ (1977). *The Restoration of the Self*. New York: International Universities Press.

_____ (1978). *The Search for the Self*, ed. P. Ornstein. New York: International Universities Press.

_____ (1984). *How Does Psychoanalysis Cure?* Chicago: University of Chicago Press.

Kohut, H., and Wolf, E. (1978). The disorders of the self and their treatment: an outline. *International Journal of Psycho-Analysis* 59:413–425.

Lichtenberg, J. (1989). *Psychoanalysis and Motivation*. Hillsdale, NJ: Analytic Press.

_____ (1991). *Self and Motivational Systems*. Hillsdale, NJ: Analytic Press.

Stern, D. (1985). *The Interpersonal World of the Infant*. New York: Basic Books.

Terman, D. (1992). Introduction. In *Progress in Self Psychology*, vol. 8, ed. A. Goldberg, p. xii. Hillsdale, NJ: Analytic Press.

Weissman, S., and Cohen, R. (1985). The parenting alliance and adolescence. *Adolescent Psychiatry* 12:24–45.

Wolf, E. (1980). On the development line of selfobject relations. In *Advances in Self Psychology*, ed. A. Goldberg, pp. 117–132. New York: International Universities Press.

_____ (1988). *Treating the Self: Elements of Clinical Self Psychology*. New York: Guilford.

_____ (1993). Disruptions of the therapeutic relationship in psychoanalysis: a view from self psychology. *International Journal of Psycho-Analysis* 74:675–687.

5

Needs, Disruptions, and the Return of Ego Instincts: Some Explicit and Implicit Aspects of Self Psychology

Discussion of Wolf's Chapter "Selfobject Experiences: Development, Psychopathology, Treatment"

Salman Akhtar, M.D.

D r. Ernest Wolf's chapter provides an up-to-date and sophisticated account of self psychology, to which he himself has made important and lasting contributions (Kohut and Wolf 1978, Wolf 1980, 1988). His discussion is lucid, well crafted, and covers a vast area involving both the developmental theory and psychoanalytic technique, especially as these are envisioned by contemporary self psychology.

SELF PSYCHOLOGY BEYOND KOHUT

Dr. Wolf begins by emphasizing that self psychology has become more refined in texture and broader in scope since its emergence with Kohut's work in the 1970s (Kohut 1971, 1977). Among the subsequent developments in self psychology, Dr. Wolf includes (1) a shift of emphasis from the self to selfobject experience, (2) a greater variety in the spectrum of needed selfobject experiences, and (3) an altered view of the mirror transference being the search for confirmatory reflection of normal well-being and not of infantile grandiosity. While Dr. Wolf does not explicitly state this, I discern two other significant advances: (1) a greater acceptance of the oedipus complex, and (2) the acknowledgment of the growth-promoting role of optimal frustration (cf. the concept of adversarial selfobject relations). Also refreshing is the attempt to clearly spell out the vicissitudes of selfobject needs through the various phases of the human life span.

All this is ample evidence that self psychology has come of age. Dr. Wolf's chapter is proof enough for the valid and useful notions self psychology has to offer us. Yet problems between mainstream psychoanalysis and self psychology (Akhtar 1984) remain. The Oedipus complex is one such area of difficulty. This psychoanalytic shibboleth has occupied varying places in self psychology. In Kohut's "classical phase," the Oedipus complex was accorded theoretical pre-eminence. In his "transitional phase" (Kohut 1971), the concept of an independent narcissistic libido nudged the Oedipus complex to a somewhat diminished, parallel position. Finally, in his "radical phase" (Kohut 1977, 1982, 1984) the Oedipus complex was relegated to the periphery.[1] This was accompanied by the sentiment, not altogether different from the one earlier voiced by Fairbairn (1952), that the Oedipus complex, far from being an organizing and ubiquitous developmental epoch, was a psychic artifact, an anomaly.

Now, sixteen years after Kohut's (1977) *Restoration of the Self,* in Dr. Wolf's paper the Oedipus complex is once again recognized and not declared as necessarily a pathological phenomenon. At the same time, this recognition seems half-hearted. Dr. Wolf says, "Self psychologists generally think that the child can traverse the oedipal experience without

---

1. I have elsewhere (Akhtar 1989) described in detail these three phases in Kohut's psychoanalytic theorizing.

permanent damage if the parental response is benignly appropriate and not neurotically reactive." Most psychoanalysts would agree with this. Potential for disagreement, however, increases when Dr. Wolf says, "Castration anxiety and penis envy, therefore, are not inescapable experiences for the child but conditional upon the individual parental and sociocultural configurations that impact on the child's development of self." I would concede that it is possible, even likely, that specific oedipal configurations, particular scenarios of unconscious fantasy, and the degrees of explicitness of related psychophysical imagery depend upon a given culture's family and a given family's culture. To suggest, however, that castration anxiety and penis envy are, in and of themselves, idiosyncratically or culturally determined is to permit culture at large an etiologic rather than pathoplastic role in the unfolding of human psychic development. This is debatable, to say the least, and psychoanalytically dubious, to say some more.

The matter of the Oedipus complex is, however, only one example of the fact that, despite recent advances, self psychology still lacks full acceptance of certain fundamental postulates of traditional psychoanalytic theory. Another example is constituted by how self psychology regards the importance of a growing child's sex. In Kohut's seminal work (especially Kohut 1977), it did not seem to have any bearing upon the child's psychic development. Dr. Wolf, in contrast, does pay attention to this crucial variable. However, he refers only to the differential parental responses needed by boys and girls in the oedipal phase. He accounts for neither the gender-determined constitutional differences affecting psychic development from the very beginning of life, nor the differences in the intrapsychic fantasy life of little boys and girls.

I can mention still more examples of such divergence from customary psychoanalytic propositions in both Dr. Wolf's chapter and the contemporary self psychology literature. This is, however, not the route I will take in this discussion. I will also avoid the oft-repeated, albeit important, criticisms leveled against self psychology: Kohut's historical solipsism (Akhtar 1988, 1989, Bacal 1987, Stein 1979), under-estimation of the limits of empathically derived knowledge (Wallerstein 1983), artificial separation of conflict and deficit (Wallerstein 1983), and overemphasis on the manifest content at the cost of hidden unconscious material (Cooper 1983). Rather than reiterate these themes, and instead of commenting upon the individual clinical illustrations, I will select two specific concepts from Dr. Wolf's chapter to highlight simul-taneously the valuable and the problematic aspects of self psychology. The first is the concept of *need* and the second that of *disruption*. After discussing them separately, I will make some concluding theoretical remarks to demonstrate the or-igin of the concepts of need and disruption in the early psy-choanalytic concept of *ego instincts* (Freud 1905, 1915a).

THE CONCEPT OF PSYCHIC NEEDS

Dr. Wolf's chapter contains the word *need* (as noun, adjective, or verb) numerous times. In contrast, it does not mention the more familiar psychoanalytic motivational concept of *wish* even once. This discrepancy is important. It highlights that what we are dealing with here is a psychology of needs and not one of wishes. I must hasten to add that I do not oppose in principle a psychology of needs. Indeed, earlier I have myself (Akhtar 1992a) proposed that a distinction between needs and wishes might be warranted. The distinction, however, is a tricky one and requires clear definitions of the two terms. Without this, further comments on Dr. Wolf's ideas might not be fruitful.

Definitions of *wish* abound in psychoanalytic literature but, in general, there seems to be a consensus that a wish is a psychic derivative of an instinctual drive that seeks gratification of the said drive in a manner that is "personal and specific" (Brenner 1982, p. 26) to that individual. The concept of a psychological *need*, however, lacks such precision. None of the major psychoanalytic glossaries (Laplanche and Pontalis, 1973, Moore and Fine, 1968, 1990, Rycroft, 1968) contains its definition. Freud himself used *wish* (*Wunsch*) more often than *need*. His most clear elucidation of *Wunsch* is in the context of the dream theory, where it seems possible to distinguish between a need and a wish. He referred to an experience of satisfaction after which the mnemic image of a particular perception remains associated

> with the memory-trace of the excitation produced by the need. As a result of the link that has been established, next time this need arises a psychical impulse will seek to re-cathect the mnemic image of the perception and revoke the perception itself, that is to say to reestablish the situation of the original satisfaction. An impulse of this kind is what we call a wish. [Freud 1900, pp. 565–566]

Freud, therefore, seems to distinguish between *need* and *wish*. Need arises from internal tension, achieves satisfaction through the specific action that procures the specific object (e.g., food). Wish, in contrast, is indissolubly bound to memory traces and is fulfilled through the hallucinatory reproduction of the perceptions that signify this satisfaction. Need is internally generated, wish is experience bound. Also, need is a more fundamental motivation, while wish is contingent upon a need; it is dubious that a wish could exist without a need. Finally, Freud implies that unlike wishes, which are subject to repression, needs cannot be repressed (Harold Blum, personal communication, May 1993). The two concepts hence are at different levels of abstraction. In all fairness, however, it should be noted that Freud often used the two terms interchangeably, employing one where the other would have seemed preferable (e.g., the wish to sleep, the need for punishment).

The distinction is clearer in the English language. Webster defines *need* as "necessity, compulsion . . . a lack of something useful . . . a condition in which there is a deficiency of something" and *wish* as "to desire, to long for, to want" (Webster's 2nd ed. 1983). Differences become readily apparent. Need is portrayed as contingent upon lack, wish is not. Need is mostly described as a noun, wish is mostly described as a verb. Need is portrayed as pressing ("compulsion"), wish has no such qualifiers. Indeed the synonyms for need in Webster are "exigency, emergency, strait, extremity, necessity, distress," even "destitution, poverty, indigence (and) penury."

For understanding the need–wish distinction, the human body, too, is an informative source. Examples of its wishes include a soft mattress to sleep upon, vanilla ice cream, a particular type of toilet, sex with a specific individual. Examples of its needs include the requirements of oxygen, sleep, food, elimination, and release from sexual tension. Once again, the distinction is apparent. Wishes are idiosyncratic, needs are universal. Frustration of the body's wishes does not cause structural damage; deprivation of its needs does.

Equipped with this metapsychological, linguistic, and somatic thesaurus, one might define *need* in the psychic realm as the requirement that (1) emanates from a state of deficit, (2) is felt with a sense of urgency, (3) is common to all human beings, and (4) if left unfulfilled, results in a structural disintegration of the mind. Its being contingent upon lack and its preservative/restorative potential vis-à-vis psychic structure lends *need* yet another quality, (5) a certain freedom from intentionality, conferring upon it an aura of justifiability.

By now it should be clear that I am quite sympathetic to Dr. Wolf's motivational emphasis upon needs. To feel recognized, accepted, validated, and affirmed do seem human needs and so are the longings to feel affiliation, rootedness, and efficacy of one's efforts. I have no disagreement with Dr. Wolf here. At the same time, I detect many unanswered questions. First, is the need–wish distinction, in the day-to-day clinical setting, to be made phenomenologically? To do so seems problematic. An inordinately entitled patient might experience his wishes as pressing needs. Another patient who has an ascetic bent might deride his needs as mere wishes. Yet another might feel secure in labeling all desires "needs" and not "wishes"; after all, having needs carries a lesser burden of intentionality. Phenomenology, therefore, does not seem a reliable guide here but what is the alternative? Second, are needs and wishes as distinct in adult life as during childhood? It seems that in the course of development, needs and wishes become condensed with each other. Also, developmental needs that have remained unmet during formative years do not result in psychic gaps or holes but in compensatory structures involving powerful affects and fantasies (Curtis 1983).

The surgical separation of needs and wishes, implicit in Dr. Wolf's approach, seems, therefore, untenable. Such separation runs contrary to the "principle of multiple function" (Waelder 1930), a central tenet of psychoanalytic theorizing. In clinical situations, therefore, the need–wish distinction will have to be a relative one at best. Some fantasy, some desire, some yearning of a patient might be viewed as predominantly need-based and others predominantly wish-based, or would be viewed as arising exclusively from one or the other motivational substrate. For instance, a narcissistic patient's idealization of his analyst would be viewed as containing both his continued need for an admirable parent and a defensive wish to ward off aggression against the undeniably imperfect analyst. A schizoid patient's withdrawal would be viewed as manifesting both his need to protect himself from the intimacy of the transference relationship and his wish to arouse curiosity and a rescue effort on the part of the analyst. And so on.

Such fluid conceptualization has significant implications for one's view of both psychic development and therapeutic technique. In the realm of development, an exclusive focus on needs tends to paint a rather passive picture of the growing child.[2] Adding the vector of wishes alters the scene altogether. Now the child appears not only in a passive receptive (need) mode but also in an active executive (wish) engagement with his or her environment. Adding the concept of wishes does not negate the structure-building role of fulfilled needs; it only questions the narrowness that results from a model emphasizing needs alone.

An even regard for needs and wishes will also enrich the analyst's technical armamentarium. Faced with a transference-based yearning, the analyst will stop short of readily seeing it as a direct replication of an unmet need from an earlier interpersonal context. The analyst will listen not only with benevolent credulousness but also with informed skepticism. Such a dual listening attitude is central to adapting a mixture of what Strenger (1989) has labeled a "romantic" and a "classical" vision of psychoanalysis. Dr. Wolf's approach is masterly in the first realm but pays insufficient attention to the latter. In agreement with Strenger, I advocate an approach of even regard for needs and wishes and, by implication, for their respective structural progenitors—deficit and conflict (see also Killingmo 1989). Such an approach, while cognizant of the patient's healthy search for affirmation, will prompt the analyst to avoid the lure of the manifest content, however

2. Self psychology does talk of a more active sort of inner motivation based upon "nuclear idealized goal structures" (Kohut 1977, p. 179) and manifesting as the individual's aspirations and ambitions. However, self psychology traces the origin of psychopathology only to the frustration of "needs," making no mention of the difficulties potentially arising from "ambitions" (e.g., too strong, contradictory, unrealistic).

poignant. It will prevent premature and linear reconstructions that often result from a countertransference-based inability to discern the elements of a "personal myth" (Kris 1956) in the formulations offered by the patient (see also Kramer and Akhtar 1988).

All in all, while the concept of need seems important in both the developmental and therapeutic context, its informative value is compromised, not enhanced, by the exclusion of wishes (and defenses against them) that invariably lie intermingled in the clinical material.

IN DEFENSE OF DISRUPTION

In his discussion of psychoanalytic treatment, Dr. Wolf describes the "disruption-restoration process." He states:

> In a smoothly proceeding psychoanalytic treatment one can observe often, perhaps always, sudden disruptions that transform a relatively harmonious working relationship between analyst and analysand—sometimes referred to as the therapeutic alliance—into an adversarial ambience . . . The disruption is ushered in when the analysand suddenly experiences the analyst as not being attuned or attentive. . . .
>
> Analysands unquestionably experience a lack of empathy and understanding. The analyst must recognize and acknowledge that because, by so doing, (1) he provides the patient with an experience of having effectively communicated to the analyst, that is, a self-enhancing experience of efficacy, and, (2) he restores the patient's experience of a selfobject bond with the analyst. . . . The acknowledgment by the analyst of his having been experienced by the analysand in such a way as to trigger the disruption usually leads to a collaborative inquiry by both into the dynamic and genetic causes of the disruption.

I agree with Dr. Wolf's statement that the disruption-restoration process during the psychoanalytic dialogue, which seems to contain echoes of the infantile "appeal cycle" described by Settlage et al. (1992), is profoundly important to understand. I also agree that the moments of disruption are often quite painful to the patient. However, in my experience, unfortunate disruptions of this sort do not happen in all analyses but only during the treatment of certain patients. It is as if there is, in such patients, a "structural turning point" (Killingmo 1989) where a conflict-based transference fades away and a deficit-based transference takes over. "Passing that point, the investigative attitude no longer matches the structural level of the patient and the analyst has to change his strategy" (Killingmo 1989, p. 74). His listening attitude should now be governed by a "romantic" and not a "classical" vision (Strenger 1989), that is, he should listen with true credulousness, temporarily suspending his customary skepticism. The choice of his interventions should also reflect his change. He should now employ plausability-rendering "affirmative interventions" and postpone meaning-seeking "interpretive interventions" to a later time when the patient has returned from the level of deficit to the level of conflict (Killingmo 1989). In essence, the analyst's technique should oscillate in accordance with the patient's level of structural organization.

Perhaps my position differs from that of Dr. Wolf only in the use of a particular psychoanalytic idiom. However, it is also likely that our differences go deeper. After all, I am not so certain about the universality of intense and painful disruptions, and I feel that the downward structural shift of the patient is complexly determined, reflecting a mix of trauma-generated psychic vulnerability and a defensive flight from the anxiety of conflict-based transferences.

More importantly, Dr. Wolf's chapter conveys the sense that disruption is something basically undesirable. In contrast, I feel that disruption, far from being an exception, is an integral aspect of both psychic development and psychoanalytic process. Let us take development first. Traced through the life span, one can observe that (1) the onset of the differentiation subphase disrupts the calm of symbiosis, and the rapprochement subphase destabilizes the euphoric self-reliance of the practicing phase proper (Mahler et al. 1975); (2) the discovery of anatomical differences between sexes (Freud 1925) puts an uncomfortable end to the ignorant bliss of the preceding era; (3) the beginning of adolescence (Blos 1967, Erikson 1950) abruptly terminates the playful equanimity of latency; and (4) the arrival of middle age, with its own characteristic psychosocial challenges (Kernberg 1980), shakes up the hitherto coherent adulthood. Psychic development throughout life seems to occur in a dialectics of "noisy" phases, which introduce new developmental tasks, and "non-noisy" phases, which synthesize, consolidate, and play out these gains (Leaff 1991, p. 205).

Disruption also appears integral to microscopic cross sections of human experience especially during the formative years. A case in point here is Pruett's (1990) elucidation of the "homeostatic" and "disruptive" attunements of parents to their growing child. Pruett has demonstrated that mothers usually *join in with the child* in his or her ongoing play, thus giving the latter a sense of continuity, validity, and harmony (homeostatic attunement). Fathers, on the contrary, characteristically disrupt the playing child's equilibrium by cajoling the child into *joining them* in a new activity (disruptive attunement). Interestingly, fathers do so only when the mother is with the child. In her absence, and especially with younger children, fathers too resort to homeostatic attunement. It is as if homeostatic attunement is a prerequisite for the disruptive attunement. Extrapolating this developmental observation to therapeutic technique, one could say that the affirmative and holding functions of the analyst must be in place in order for his interpretive efforts to be fruitful.

The homeostatic attunement has affirming qualities, nec-

essary for the consolidation of self experience. The disruptive
attunement has enhancing potential, necessary for the expansion of the self experience. The influence of both attunements
is additive and contributes to the fluid solidity of the self
experience. Indeed, the two attunements might even be necessary for the two sides of identity—subjective self-sameness
and self objectification (Erikson 1956, Lichtenstein 1963)—to
develop.

Developmentally speaking, therefore, disruption seems
not an exception but a rule. The same appears true of psychoanalytic treatment. The psychoanalytic process, viewed long-
itudinally, is a lyrical but long sentence, punctuated by many
commas and semicolons. Some of these disruptions are extra-
neous though no less integral, for example, analyst's vacations. Others are more or less unavoidable artifacts, for
example, analyst's lateness or illness. Still others, perhaps the
more significant destabilizations, are inherent in the very
nature of the analytic process. For instance, moving from a
sitting position during the initial evaluation to lying on the
couch at the beginning of analysis causes a destabilization
based upon the economic changes in optimal distance (Akhtar
1992b, Bouvet 1958, Escoll 1992), visual input (Wright
1991), and stability of object constancy (Frank 1992). Then
the development of transference neurosis destabilizes the
holding and empathic ambience of the beginning phase. Still
later, with the interpretive working through of major transferences, termination-phase phenomena begin to appear, at
times catching both the patient and the analyst by surprise.
Negative therapeutic reactions with their diverse underlying
dynamics are also moments when destabilization appears in
place of the expected stabilization and advance.

Cross-sectionally, the very moment of interpretation is a
disrupting one insofar as it expands the patient's knowledge,
bringing to his or her awareness something new to consider.
Indeed, psychoanalysis with its emphasis on interpretation

might be largely viewed as a destabilizing treatment. [Dr. Eric Lager's ideas (personal communication) have, in part, shaped my thinking vis-à-vis this particular issue.] Psychotherapy, with its support of the existing defenses, might be viewed as a stabilizing one. Actually, psychoanalytic treatment, more so of some patients than of others, oscillates between stabilizing and destabilizing moments, or to extend Pruett's (1990) developmental observations, between homeostatic and disruptive attunements. Wright's (1991) notion about there being "maternal" and "paternal" features to the psychoanalytic technique addresses this issue. Killingmo's (1989) suggestion that "the analyst should be in a state of constant receptivity for oscillation between the two strategic positions" (p. 74) of offering "affirmative interventions" and "interpretive interventions" speaks to this very point.

In sum, therefore, I do not believe that disruption is an exception, something to be avoided in either developmental or therapeutic context. To the contrary, disruptive phenomena are integral to the developmental and therapeutic processes, both of which unfold in the dialectic of stabilization, affirmation, and synthesis on the one hand, and, disruption, new challenges, and surprise on the other hand.

CONCLUDING REMARKS

Dr. Wolf has presented us with an elegant model of mind, psychopathology, and its amelioration. At the risk of oversimplification, this model can be summarized as follows. The growing child has certain needs that must be met in order to assure sound development. If the environment fails to meet these needs, a state of deficit results. Growth continues but the effects of this deficit remain. These effects lead the individual to seek psychotherapeutic help. During treatment, the unmet needs get reactivated. When the analyst fails to meet them, or at least to appreciate their existence and their validity, a disruption ensues. If now the analyst can acknowledge that he has been experienced by the analysand in such a way as to trigger a disruption, it leads to their collaborative inquiry into the dynamic and genetic causes of such disruption. Cycles of this sort are repeated with deepening insight, reconstructions, internalizations, and enhanced solidity of the analysand's self.

All four constituents of this model—deficit, need, disruption, and restoration—are useful constructs. None of them, however, can be viewed in isolation. Deficit does not exist apart from conflict. Needs cannot be surgically separated from wishes. Disruption is not only a painful experience of one's needs—either from parents or from the analyst—not being met, it is also an integral aspect of the developmental and the analytic processes. Restoration, in the form of empathic affirmation of subjective experience, is helpful and soothing but does not replace interpretation. Deficit, need, disruption, and restoration are valuable concepts only when tempered by alternate, additional, and competing hypotheses.

The fundamental motivation in this model is that of *need,* specifically the need to preserve (and under threatening circumstances, restore) psychic structure and its smooth functioning. The self psychology concept of such self-preservative need, even if curiously divorced from the human body, seems nothing but a disguised resurrection of the early Freudian notion of ego instincts. These were directed at self-preservation, fulfilled nonsexual needs, operated under reality principle, and carried an energy of their own that was not libido but "interest" (Freud 1905, 1910, 1915a). All these are also the features of the psychological needs that form the focus of self psychology. What then is the problem?

In moving from his first dual instinct theory (Freud 1905, 1915a) of sexual and ego instincts to his second dual instinct theory (Freud 1920) of life and death instincts, Freud relegated ego instincts to the domain of life instinct. Regrettably, this move led to a gradual loss of conceptual zeal about ego instincts. Motivations, psychopathology, and transferences were infrequently traced back to thwarted self-preservative tendencies. The concept of ego instincts became "repressed." Yet, like the repressed, which exerts a "continuous pressure in the direction of the conscious" (Freud 1915b, p. 151), it kept seeking readmission in the main corpus of the psychoanalytic thought. Winnicott (1965) spoke of "ego needs." Modell (1975) argued for "quieter" instincts, not associated with id function and accounting for the development of attachment and object relations. Casement (1991) reformulated the concept as "growth needs," distinguishing them from "libidinal demands." The thinking behind these diverse but overlapping concepts also found a counterpart in the broadening view of psychoanalytic process. Loewald (1960) conceptualized the analytic situation as a developmental one and was supported by many others (Robbins in Escoll 1977, Fleming 1975). Also pertinent in this context is Abrams's (1978) concept of "developmental interpretation," which brings an unconscious progressive potential into consciousness and thus facilitates the emergence of experiential building blocks necessary for development.

Among the varying revivals of the concept of ego instincts, self psychology occupies a prominent, albeit curious, place. On the one hand, its distance from classical metapsychology precludes the acknowledgment of its having resurrected ego instincts. On the other hand, it might be the most methodical and far reaching, though single-minded, elaboration of the heuristic and technical value of the ego instinct concept.

Freud once compared the repressed to a heckler who upon being removed from an auditorium keeps banging on its doors. The ego instinct concept has been such a heckler. Perhaps it is time that we let the heckler back in and listen to him. At the same time, his readmission should not diminish our regard for those already present in the audience: intrapsychic conflict, overdetermination, unconscious fantasy, Oedipus complex, and, in the very front row, the two instinctual drives of sex and aggression.

REFERENCES

Abrams, S. (1978). The teaching and learning of psychoanalytic developmental psychology. *Journal of the American Psychoanalytic Association* 26:387–406.

Akhtar, S. (1984). Self psychology versus mainstream psychoanalysis. *Contemporary Psychiatry* 3:113–117.

——— (1988). Some reflections on the theory of psychopathology and personality development in Kohut's self psychology. In *New Concepts in Psychoanalytic Psychotherapy*, ed. J. M. Ross and W. A. Myers, pp. 227–252. Washington, DC: American Psychiatric Press.

——— (1989). Kohut and Kernberg: a critical comparison. In *Self Psychology: Comparisons and Contrasts*, ed. D. W. Detrick and S. P. Detrick, pp. 329–363. Hillsdale, NJ: Analytic Press.

——— (1992a). *Broken Structures: Severe Personality Disorders and Their Treatment*. Northvale, NJ: Jason Aronson.

——— (1992b). Tethers, orbits, and invisible fences: clinical, developmental, sociocultural, and technical aspects of optimal distance. In *When the Body Speaks: Psychological Meanings in Kinetic Clues*, ed. S. Kramer and S. Akhtar, pp. 21–57. Northvale, NJ: Jason Aronson.

Bacal, H. A. (1987). British object relations theorists and self psychology: some critical reflections. *International Journal of Psycho-Analysis* 58:209–233.

Blos, P. (1967). The second individuation process of adolescence. *Psychoanalytic Study of the Child* 22:162–186. New York: International Universities Press.

Bouvet, M. (1958). Technical variations and the concept of distance. *International Journal of Psycho-Analysis* 39:211–221.

Brenner, C. (1982). *The Mind In Conflict*. New York: International Universities Press.

Casement, P. J. (1991). *Learning from the Patient*. New York: Guilford.

Cooper, A. M. (1983). The place of self psychology in the history of depth psychology. In *The Future of Psychoanalysis*, ed. A. Goldberg, pp. 3–17. New York: International Universities Press.

Curtis, H. C. (1983). Book review of *The Search for the Self: Selected Writings of Heinz Kohut*, ed. P. H. Ornstein. *Journal of the American Psychoanalytic Association* 31:272–285.

Erikson, E. H. (1950). *Childhood and Society*. New York: W. W. Norton.

——— (1956). The problem of ego identity. In *Identity and the Life Cycle*, pp. 104–164. New York: International Universities Press, 1959.

Escoll, P. J. (1977). Panel report: the contribution of psychoanalytic developmental concepts to adult analysis. *Journal of the American Psychoanalytic Association* 25:219–234.

_____ (1992). Vicissitudes of optimal distance through the life cycle. In *When the Body Speaks: Psychological Meanings in Kinetic Clues*, ed. S. Kramer and S. Akhtar, pp. 59–87. Northvale, NJ: Jason Aronson.

Fairbairn, W. R. D. (1952). *Psychoanalytic Studies of the Personality*. London: Tavistock.

Fleming, J. (1975). Some observations on object constancy in the psychoanalysis of adults. *Journal of the American Psychoanalytic Association* 23:743–759.

Frank, A. (1992). A problem with the couch: incapacities and conflicts. In *When the Body Speaks: Psychological Meanings in Kinetic Clues*, ed. S. Kramer and S. Akhtar, pp. 89–112. Northvale, NJ: Jason Aronson.

Freud, S. (1900). Interpretation of dreams. *Standard Edition* 4,5:1–626.

_____ (1905). Three essays on the theory of sexuality. *Standard Edition* 7:135–243.

_____ (1910). The psychoanalytic view of psychogenic disturbances of vision. *Standard Edition* 11:209–218.

_____ (1915a). Instincts and their vicissitudes. *Standard Edition* 14:105–216.

_____ (1915b). Regression. *Standard Edition* 14:141–158.

_____ (1920). Beyond the pleasure principle. *Standard Edition* 18:7–64.

_____ (1925). Some psychical consequences of the anatomical distinction between the sexes. *Standard Edition* 19:243–258.

Kernberg, O. F. (1980). *Internal World and External Reality*. New York: Jason Aronson.

Killingmo, B. (1989). Conflict and deficit: implications for technique. *International Journal of Psycho-Analysis* 70:65–79.

Kohut, H. (1971). *The Analysis of the Self*. New York: International Universities Press.

_____ (1977). *The Restoration of the Self*. New York: International Universities Press.

_____ (1982). Introspection, empathy and the semi-circle of mental health. *International Journal of Psycho-Analysis* 63:395–407.

_____ (1984). *How Does Analysis Cure?* Chicago: University of Chicago Press.

Kohut, H., and Wolf, E. S. (1978). The disorders of the self and their treatment: an outline. *International Journal of Psycho-Analysis* 59:413–425.

Kramer, S., and Akhtar, S. (1988). The developmental context of internalized preoedipal object relations: clinical applications of Mahler's theory of symbiosis and separation individuation. *Psychoanalytic Quarterly* 57:547–576.

Kris, E. (1956). The personal myth: a problem in psychoanalytic technique. *Journal of the American Psychoanalytic Association* 4:653–681.

Laplanche, J., and Pontalis, J. B. (1973). *The Language of Psychoanalysis*, trans. D. Nicholson-Smith. New York: W. W. Norton.

Leaff, L. A. (1991). Separation-individuation and adolescence with special reference to character formation. In *Beyond the Symbiotic Orbit: Advances in Separation-Individuation Theory—Essays in honor of Selma Kramer, M.D.*, ed. S. Akhtar and H. Parens, pp. 189–208. Hillsdale, NJ: Analytic Press.

Lichtenstein, H. (1963). The dilemma of human identity: notes on self-transformation, self-objectivation and metamorphosis. *Journal of the American Psychoanalytic Association* 11:173–223.

Loewald, H. W. (1960). On the therapeutic action of psychoanalysis. *International Journal of Psycho-Analysis* 41:16–33.

Mahler, M. S., Pine, F., and Bergman, A. (1975). *The Psychological Birth of the Human Infant.* New York: Basic Books.

Modell, A. (1975). The ego and the id. *International Journal of Psycho-Analysis* 56:57–68.

Moore, B. E., and Fine, B. D., eds. (1968). *A Glossary of Psychoanalytic Terms and Concepts.* New York: American Psychoanalytic Association.

——— (1990). *Psychoanalytic Terms and Concepts.* New York: American Psychoanalytic Association.

Pruett, K. (1990). *The impact of involved fatherhood on child development: research and clinical perspectives.* Paper presented at the October scientific meeting of the Philadelphia Psychoanalytic Society.

Rycroft, C. (1968). *A Critical Dictionary of Psychoanalysis.* Middlesex, England: Penguin Books.

Settlage, C. F., Bemesderfer, S., Rosenthal, J., et al. (1991). The appeal cycle in early mother–child interaction: the nature and implications of a finding from developmental research. *Journal of the American Psychoanalytic Association* 39:987–1014.

Stein, M. R. (1979). Book review of *The Restoration of the Self. Journal of the American Psychoanalytic Association* 27:665–680.

Strenger, C. (1989). The classic and romantic visions in psychoanalysis. *International Journal of Psycho-Analysis* 70:595–610.

Waelder, R. (1930). The principle of multiple function; observations on overdetermination. *Psychoanalytic Quarterly* 5:45–62.

Wallerstein, R. S. (1983). Self psychology and "classical" psychoanalytic psychology: the nature of their relationship. In *The Future of Psychoanalysis,* ed. A. Goldberg, pp. 19–63. New York: International Universities Press.

Winnicott, D. W. (1965). *Maturational Processes and the Facilitating Environment.* London: Hogarth.

Wolf, E. (1980). On the developmental line of selfobject relations. In *Advances in Self Psychology,* ed. A. Goldberg, pp. 117–132. New York: International Universities Press.

——— (1988). *Treating the Self: Elements of Clinical Self Psychology.* New York: Guilford.

Wright, K. (1991). *Vision and Separation: Between Mother and Baby.* Northvale, NJ: Jason Aronson.

6

Mahler and Kohut:
A Comparative View

Howard B. Levine, M.D.

" . . . without disagreement psychoanalytic theory
would be dead."
(Joseph Sandler 1983)

In an address to the 1983 International Psychoanalytical
Congress in Madrid, Joseph Sandler (1983) noted that many
psychoanalytic writings contain "an implicit unconscious as-
sumption . . . that our theory should . . . be a body of ideas
that is essentially complete and organized, with each part
being fully integrated with every other." According to this
view, disagreements that exist between contending theories
or tensions that arise between incongruent parts of a given
theory are conceptual imperfections in need of corrective
elaboration or emendation. For adherents of this position, the
ultimate goal of psychoanalysis would seem to be the creation
of a unitary and coherent theory, one whose pieces begin with
the works of Freud and fit neatly together like a jigsaw puzzle.

There is much to be valued in this position. At its most

constructive, it may be used to support and protect fundamental psychoanalytic concepts and propositions, relating
new developments in our field to the writings of Freud and
other core contributors. This same position, however, may
also be misused in the service of idealizing or authoritarian
trends. These may obstruct scientific inquiry and reduce le-
gitimate discourse to sectarian quarrels about whether a given
theory is "right" or "wrong" or whether or not something is
or is not "psychoanalysis."

As a corrective, Sandler (1983) encouraged the adoption
of a *developmental-historical* perspective in which theoretical
strain is understood to be inevitable. Considered in this light,
psychoanalytic theory appears as a

> body of thought which has been in a state of continuous
> organic development since the beginning. As ideas have de-
> veloped on one front, so there have been repercussions in
> other areas, and theoretical strain has constantly been—and is
> being—generated. Every new definition, every new gain in
> precision, puts pressure on other aspects of theory. [Sandler
> 1983, p. 35]

From this perspective, even our most fundamental concepts,
such as narcissism, fantasy, trauma, resistance, or transference, may be seen to possess a relative degree of fluidity over
time. They expand, evolve, and support multiple connotations, even multiple meanings, which are often heavily dependent upon the contexts in which they appear.

The expectation that inconsistency and strain are inevitable consequences of elaborations and refinements of our
analytic constructs can free us from the confines of an idealized or unitary view of psychoanalysis and place us instead in
the position of trying to understand what clinical or theoretical problems a given contributor was attempting to address
and why a given formulation was being advanced. Similarly,

in considering clinical reports, a developmental-historical position may help us avoid the pitfall of debating whether or not the material offered illustrates the presence of *the* psychoanalytic process (e.g., "Is it *really* psychoanalysis or *only* psychotherapy?") and move us instead toward the far more useful and interesting question of how to understand and conceptualize the unique analytic process that is being presented.

It is the developmental-historical position that allows for the possibility of a truly *comparative* exploration within psychoanalysis, and it is from this perspective that I would like to address my discussion. In particular, I will focus on how the work of Mahler and Kohut represents two different attempts to respond to the need within psychoanalysis to refine our concepts of the object and the real object relationship, and the roles that these play in normal and pathological development and in the analytic treatment process.

MAHLER AND KOHUT:
TWO DIFFERENT APPROACHES

Comparing the work of Mahler and Kohut is not an easy task. In the early 1970s, Mahler attempted to engage Kohut in a discussion about the similarities and differences of their views (Shane and Shane 1989). Kohut (1980) responded by saying that he saw each of them as "digging tunnels from different directions into the same area of the mountain." Taken at face value, we might assume that this remark indicated an affinity between Kohut's reconstructive focus on the development and function of the self and Mahler's (1979, Mahler et al. 1975) prospective, infant observational investigation of the elaboration of identity. In her *Memoirs* (Mahler/Stepansky 1988), Mahler wrote, "For me, . . . the general problem of identity, and especially the way in which one arrives at a sense of self, has always been primary" (pp. 136–137).

Alternatively, Kohut's response might have reflected the fact that they shared a common interest in the investigation of self-esteem and in the origins, development, and functioning of the structures that continue to regulate self-esteem throughout the life cycle; that parallels might exist between the later vicissitudes of an unsuccessfully negotiated symbiotic stage and those transactions of incompletely felt separation that Kohut (1971) called "merger transferences"; or that there was some overlap between the application of Mahler's theory of separation-individuation to the treatment of borderline and other primitive personality disorders (e.g., Mahler 1971, Settlage 1977) and Kohut's clinical contributions to the treatment of what he came to refer to as "the disorders of the self" (Kohut and Wolf 1978).

However, by 1980, when Kohut first mentioned their exchange,—three years after the publication of *The Restoration of the Self* (Kohut 1977)—their theoretical aims were already quite different. Kohut's work had gone far beyond his initial attempts (e.g., Kohut 1966, 1968) to work out the description of the narcissistic transferences and the treatment of the narcissistic personality disorders. In this earlier phase, which he later referred to as "the psychology of the self in the narrow sense" (Kohut 1971), his contributions were subsumed under the aegis of ego psychology and the structural theory. Once Kohut (1977) proposed the concept of the supraordinate self and launched self psychology in its broad sense, his program shifted from an attempt to clarify the development, psychopathology, and treatment of a particular subset of clinical disorders within the then-dominant paradigm of psychoanalysis (i.e., psychoanalysis as a theory of conflict) to a redefinition and replacement of that paradigm with a theory of deficit.

What remained central to both phases of Kohut's work was (1) the proposition that what the narcissistic, or self disordered, or, later (Kohut 1984), any patient needs is *"an actual behavior by the real person of the analyst"* (Friedman 1980, italics added), and (2) the commitment to study, with exquisite sensitivity and in microscopic detail, in the patient's childhood, current life, and, most importantly, in relation to the analyst, the vicissitudes of the wishes for, the defenses against, the attempts to secure, and the consequences of the failure to obtain this actual behavior. The conceptual language with which Kohut described these processes included terms such as empathy and failures of empathy, narcissistic or selfobject transferences, and relationships, fragmentation, and cohesion of the self, and so forth.

In contrast to Kohut, Mahler was a developmentalist, who, through direct observation of infants and toddlers, sought to advance our understanding of the complexities of early (preoedipal) development and psychic structure formation. The importance to her research of the real object (i.e., the mother) and the actual external (mother–child) object relationship is self-evident. In assessing the implications of Mahler's contributions to the psychoanalytic treatment of adults, Kramer and Akhtar (1988) wrote: "By highlighting the essentially dyadic nature of early object relations, Mahler's developmental theory . . . draws sharper attention to the dyadic and diatrophic nature of the analytic relationship" (p. 570). Thus, Mahler's work stands in close connection to that of many other mainstream contributors to psychoanalysis, such as Loewald (1960), Gitelson (1962), Zetzel (1965), Blum (1971), Fleming (1972, 1975), Greenacre (1975), and Settlage (1989), each of whom believed that the remobilization of previously arrested development is an integral feature and powerful therapeutic force within the psychoanalytic process. As we shall see, the assertion that thwarted developmental tendencies can resume in the context of a particular kind or quality of external object relationship is also essential to Kohut's conceptualization of the selfobject and to his final (Kohut 1984) views on the mutative role of empathy in the therapeutic process.

Despite the pioneering innovations of her work, Mahler's formulations remained clearly within the confines of
mainstream psychoanalytic theory. She attempted to preserve
and enhance drive theory, even as she enlarged upon it, so as
to better include and account for the early and ongoing importance of the external object and its internal representations.
Mahler's sensitivity to recognizing the value and necessity of
this theoretical elaboration was no doubt determined in part
by two contrasting experiences that she had undergone
during her formative years as a physician and by her ill-fated,
first training analysis with Helene Deutsch, whom she found
unfriendly and remote. She recalled:

> The ethos of antiseptic detachment from patient care pre-
> scribed by the Vienna Psychoanalytic Institute [at which
> Deutsch was a training analyst and Mahler her unhappy can-
> didate/analysand] ran counter to everything I had learned and
> experienced as a pediatrician. I had seen, in von Pirquet's
> clinic, how devastating a sterile, detached approach to sick
> children could be; conversely, I had seen in Moll's [pediatric]
> institute how therapeuticallly potent an approach of loving
> engagement could be with equally sick children. [Mahler/
> Stepansky 1988, p. 82]

At an even earlier point in her life, when Mahler was
a student in Budapest, she had come under the influence
of Ferenczi and his analytic colleagues. Despite her youth,
they included her in their circle and treated her with respect.
The influence of their ideas upon Mahler can be measured
by the esteem in which she continued to hold them, long after
she, herself, had achieved a position of preeminence within the
psychoanalytic community:

> The influential Hungarian analysts with whom I mingled . . .
> —Ferenczi, Herman, Bak, Benedek—made a very special con-

tribution to analysis. . . . The whole idea of the mother–infant dual unity, for example, originates in their theoretical and clinical perspectives. This developmental viewpoint did not gain expression in the German or Viennese psychoanalytic literature of the time. It is not even found in the later work of Anna Freud. . . . [While] the intrapsychic *is* the main thing, . . . I have undertaken to show over a lifetime of research and writing, [that] the intrapsychic only evolves out of the differentiation from the initially undifferentiated matrix of mother and child. [Mahler/Stepansky 1988, pp. 15–16]

In contrast to the direction that Kohut ultimately chose, Mahler's work "provided a further explanatory model, *complementary to psychosexual theory*, of early infantile development, the inevitable specific conflicts this line of development brings, and their derivatives in adult character and psychopathology" (Kramer and Akhtar 1988, p. 55, italics added). Thus, we can only regret Kohut's (1980) decision not to elaborate more fully upon his own view of the similarities and differences between his work and that of Mahler, and note that his inclination to leave the matter unexplained was consistent with his expressed wish to insulate his ideas from parallel or preceding concepts in the work of others, so that self psychology might have the freest reign in which to develop outside of what he must have felt to be the co-opting and constraining influences of rival psychoanalytic theories.

HISTORICAL BACKDROP

While recognizing the significance of this major point of divergence, it is worth reflecting on the historical climate in which the views of Mahler and Kohut developed. For it is here that important correspondences in their work may be discerned. To be sure, upon the closest examination, these correspondences can be seen to differ in some of their fine points, and these differences will be of particular concern to those who see themselves as advocates of one or another rival school of psychoanalytic thought. In regard to such partisan feelings, Wallerstein (1988) noted the almost religious zeal with which we can find ourselves defending our particular metapsychologies—this in contrast to the more scientific attitudes that we are likely to adopt in relation to our more congruent, validatable, and experience-near *clinical* theories: "Our different and distinguishing positions . . . [are] metaphors . . . which . . . give a sense of coherence or closure to our psychological understandings. . . . They are our pluralistic *psychoanalytic articles of faith* [and are] essentially beyond the realm of empirical study and scientific process" (p. 17, italics added).

Both Mahler and Kohut were subject to the problems and opportunities that arose in the wake of Freud's introduction of ego psychology and its elaboration by many contributors, especially Heinz Hartmann (1939, 1964) and his co-workers. Each was influenced by an ambience in which psychoanalytic interest inevitably became centered upon the early development of the ego, its origins in preoedipal object relations, and the evolution and functioning of the processes and structures that governed internalization, adaptation, and psychic regulation. Clinically, these developments supported and were driven by the extension of psychoanalytic treatment to increasingly more complex and sicker categories of patients, the so-called widening scope of indications for psychoanalytic therapy (Stone 1954). It was in this context that the contributions of Mahler and Kohut evolved.

The shift to ego psychology, with its emphasis on adaptation (Hartmann 1939), had exposed the extent to which psychoanalysis, in its urgent, even exuberant, rush to elaborate upon the implications of psychic reality and the vicissitudes of instinctual development, had underemphasized and, at times, neglected the roles of actual experience and the object. This was true for both the real, external object and its internalized representation, in development, psychoanalytic theory, and even clinical practice. (I have discussed this else-where [Levine 1990] in relation to actual childhood sexual trauma and incest.) In the clinical sphere, this relative lag in theoretical development produced a concomitant set of prob-lems with which we are familiar today, because they define many of the issues that we still struggle with on the cutting edge of clinical theory and psychoanalytic technique. These include (1) a conceptualization of the interactive, transactional, and intersubjective dimensions of the analytic relationship; (2) the extent to which relational factors (vis-à-vis primary ob-jects) contribute to pathogenesis and (vis-à-vis the therapeutic relationship) to the therapeutic impact of psychoanalytic ther-apy; and (3) the role of reality in pathogenesis and analytic treatment, including the nature of the analyst's real participa-tion in the analytic process and in the patient's processes of state regulation and homeostasis.

The latter is particularly important to a consideration of Kohut's work, because, at its most fundamental, self psy-chology is a *psychology of homeostasis* (Friedman 1980, Levine 1983). That is, the narrative story lines of a self psychological analysis tell of the individual's adaptive struggles as his/her needs for organization, modulation, and stimulation are ex-pressed and played out in the vicissitudes of the analyst–patient relationship. For Kohut, these needs are analogous, if not identical, to similar needs that existed in relation to the primary objects of infancy and childhood, and that went unmet because of some failure of the child's environment. The fact that these needs persist into adulthood is a presumed indication not only of that early environmental failure, but of the resultant relative absence or immaturity of internal, psy-chic, self-regulating structures. Hence the term *deficit* and the emphasis ultimately placed by Kohut (1977, 1984) on em-

pathy and the internalization of new psychic structures in
analysis, via a process he called "transmuting internalization,"
as curative factors in psychoanalysis.

TECHNICAL IMPLICATIONS

The concept of empathy occupies a central place in Kohut's
formulations, because its presence or absence will determine
whether the outcome of actual developmental or psychoanalytic interactions will be growth enhancing or traumatic.
What has been confusing to many clinicians is the dual sense in
which Kohut has used this term. On the one hand, particularly
in his earlier work, empathy signified a way of understanding
the patient's experience from the patient's point of view. It
was an act of perception that enabled the analyst to see the uses
to which he/she was being put in the narcissistic (selfobject)
transference (Levine 1983). Insofar as the results of this perception informed the analyst's interpretations, then the patient could feel understood in a way that was unique, unifying
to a sense of self and individuality, esteem building, and so on.

In Kohut's (1977, 1984) later work, however, empathy
became more than a listening stance or an act of perception. It
took on connotations of being a particular *quality of relationship*
that had a mutative therapeutic impact upon the patient,
above and beyond that produced by insight. Thus, Kohut
(1984) conceived of the therapeutic process as consisting of
two linked phases. In one, that of "understanding," the analyst "verbalizes to the patient that he has grasped what the
patient feels; he describes the patient's inner state to the patient, thus demonstrating to him that . . . another person has
been able to experience . . . what he himself has experienced"
(pp. 176–177). In the other, that of "explanation," the intensity of the "archaic bond of an identity of inner experiences"
(p. 184) that has been established by the communication of the

analyst's understanding is lessened, as the genetic/dynamic meanings of the patient's experiences are reconstructed.

According to Kohut, "it is the empathic bond and its continual repair by empathic understanding that does the curing: [for the patient,] being understood is a maturing environment. . . . Explanation . . . is useful mainly because it helps to sustain [and demonstrate to the patient] the empathic bond" (Friedman 1986, p. 327). I would add that explanation, and the sense of knowing that it brings, also helps the analyst to persevere and sustain his/her self in the face of sometimes turbulent and difficult interactions with the patient.

In his final formulation, Kohut (1984) summarized the matter as follows:

> A successful analysis is one in which the analysand's formerly archaic needs for the responses of archaic selfobjects are superseded by the experience of the availability of empathic resonance, the major constituent of the sense of security in adult life. Increased ability to verbalize, broadened insight, greater autonomy of ego functions, and increased control over impulsiveness may accompany these gains, but they are not the essence of cure. A treatment will be successful because . . . an analysand was able to reactivate, in a selfobject transference, the needs of a self that had been thwarted in childhood. In the analytic situation, these reactivated needs were kept alive and exposed, time and again, to the vicissitudes of optimal frustrations until the patient ultimately acquired [via transmuting internalization] the reliable ability to sustain his self with the aid of selfobject resources available in his adult surroundings. According to self psychology, then, the essence of the psychoanalytic cure resides in a patient's newly acquired ability to identify and seek out appropriate selfobjects . . . as they present themselves in his realistic surroundings and to be sustained by them. [p. 77]

What Kohut seems to be reaching for in this description is a greater emphasis on some actual quality of analyst–patient

interaction as the motor force that drives the development of
new psychic structure via the process of (transmuting) internalization. Perhaps this actual quality is related to the subtle
interplay of disappointment and relief that accompanies the
patient's experience of being empathically understood and yet
not fully enmeshed with the analyst in a truly inseparable state
of archaic merger.

Kohut's final position is clear. It is not simply the provision of knowledge, the insight, in the interpretation that is
curative. Rather, it is the analyst's empathic relationship to the
patient, which either creates or reflects the existence of a
particular kind of relationship between analyst and patient.
This relationship is one in which the patient's needs are seen
and responded to as comprehensible, developmentally progressive, and therefore justified. It is this that Kohut believes
drives the therapeutic process.

Seen in this way, it is understandable, even inevitable,
that Kohut's claims for self psychology should raise questions
about the meaning of the analyst's attempts to maintain a
stance of abstinence and neutrality, and the extent to which
real, relational forces contribute to the therapeutic impact of
psychoanalysis. It is the relative role of insight versus interaction as a therapeutic factor that inheres in the ongoing
confusion and debate about the nature, action, and role of
empathy in Kohut's formulations of the therapeutic process.

From the patient's side, the unremitting search for func-
tional replacements for absent or immature self-regulating
structures—that is, the search for real external object relationships (the so-called selfobject)—motivates behavior and,
along with the defenses against the unalloyed expression of
these (selfobject) needs, defines character pathology. From the
analyst's side,

> [the] unqualified appreciation of the value and necessity of the
> patient's strivings, [the search for] the reasonableness of the

patient's attitude and, if possible, the inevitable claim or wish that it implements, . . . conveys to the patient that his frustrated wishes are pointed towards growth [and] makes it possible for the patient to take up again the differentiation and integration of his needs. . . . What distinguishes Kohut's approach is his insistence that the patient is differentiating and integrating his aspirations in the very act of exercising them on the analyst. [Friedman 1980, p. 415]

In its most general sense, then, self psychology is a particular adaptive, object relational, and developmental point of view applied to the theory of therapy. Its tenets rest heavily upon the organizing, growth enhancing, and sustaining qualities of the actual external object relationship (the self-selfobject relationship) and the internal, self-regulating uses to which they are put. Its theories of pathogenesis, structural diagnosis, therapeutic interaction, and therapeutic change are inextricably connected to the success or failure of the environmental provision of particular kinds of actual object relationships and their internalization.

While not going nearly so far as Kohut in the direction of a radical break with classical conflict theory, Mahler's contributions have enriched our clinical repertoire in ways that are analogous to his. By working out a phenomenology of preoedipal development, Mahler brought specific analytic attention to bear on the residues of preoedipal developmental conflicts that inevitably appear in the analyses of neurotic, as well as narcissistic, borderline, and other primitive personality types. As a result of her work, these object relational conflicts have been seen to be more clearly worthy of interpretive attention in their own right, rather than being viewed only as regressive avoidances of oedipal configurations. That is, Mahler did for preoedipal object relationships and their attendant conflicts what Kohut did for the narcissistic transferences.

In sharpening our sense of the adult vicissitudes of early

development, Mahler also helped classical analysts recognize the ways in which the psychoanalytic process re-creates and even embodies a developmental process. The latter is true

> especially in those psychoanalyses which achieve a resolution of analyzable preoedipal conflicts and thereby foster movement from immature, dyadic, to complex triadic object relationships. The analysis of unresolved separation-individuation conflicts facilitates the establishment of an analyzable oedipal transference neurosis. This, for many patients, is a major developmental step forward. [Kramer and Akhtar 1988, p. 572).

Clinical reports in the analytic literature (e.g., Fleming 1975, Kramer 1979, 1990) indicate the extent to which the patient's developmental consolidation within the analysis does not occur by virtue of interpretation alone. A particular form of object relationship with the analyst often appears to be a necessary, although not sufficient, concomitant to the resolution of derivatives of preoedipal conflicts related to the process of separation-individuation. The presence of this interactional contribution to therapeutic change is sometimes obscured in case reports, where the emphasis may be placed instead upon the analyst's attempts to reconstruct (interpret) for the patient the nature of the particular relationship that is being played out. For example, the relationship may mirror some variant of a rapprochement crisis in which the patient's negativity or aggression may reflect more than the patient's anxiety-driven resistances or aggressive-drive derivatives. Rather, negativity or aggression may also serve the purposes of solidifying the patient's sense of separation and boundaries or of denying the wishes and allaying the fears of being swooped back up into the analyst/mother's symbiotic orbit.

Kramer (1979), for example, described the importance of

the analyst's fine-tuning his degree of participation and intervention to the developmental needs of the patient, noting that "much like the mother of a rapprochement subphase child, the analyst had to be available but had to be careful not to 'shadow,' to be aware of the patient's conflict between the wish to manage by herself and the wish to partake in the mother's omnipotence" (p. 251) and so had to modulate his behavior and technical stance accordingly.

In another case, Fleming (1975) was faced with a patient who suffered from intense separation anxiety and impaired object constancy. She encouraged him to try to deal with his anxiety about her absence by free associating and reporting the results to her in their subsequent sessions. In the course of attempting to do this, the patient established an unconscious link between his activity and Fleming's existence, thereby strengthening his capacity to evoke his memory of her via the (magical) gestures of doing what she had instructed him to do and thinking about what he would tell her. Ultimately, this process helped him to develop a more secure and abiding internalized representation of her presence, strengthening his sense of object constancy. In characterizing this phase of their work, Fleming (1975) wrote:

> The first step for the analyst is to try to make a diagnosis of the developmental level of the patient's ego state and assessment of his level of object need. Once such a diagnosis is made, technical responses [other than interpretations] congruent with that need can be compared with optimal object responses that facilitate normal development outside of the therapeutic situation. When this can be achieved, developmental arrests due to early object deprivation are interrupted; the derailed developmental processes can be set in motion again; and the resistances to the "separations" (changes) that all efforts at separation-individuation are heir to can be worked through in a therapeutic experience which is also developmental. [p. 749]

Although the nature of the salutary form of object relationship described by classical analysts such as Kramer and Fleming may be quite different from that described by self psychologists, the description of developmental gains occurring in the context of a particular form of actual object relationship mobilized within the transference has obvious parallels with the work of Kohut. Where Mahler and her colleagues differ from Kohut is in being clear that the provision of a particular kind of growth-promoting relationship is only an adjunctive therapeutic factor in the analysis and so can never replace interpretation. They add this caution:

> The therapist must avoid the pitfall of indefinitely accepting the patient's transference expectation for purposes of meeting an early object need. Such a compensatory supply has value in the beginning, but indefinite acceptance fails to help the patient differentiate the past from the present and can reinforce the state of arrested development in the ego and self-system. [Fleming 1972, p. 44]

In addition, a theory of therapeutic interaction that consistently views the patient's distress as secondary to the failure of the object and not internally driven possesses the potential drawback of "blaming the object" and seeming to absolve the patient from all personal responsibility for his/her actions. (See Adler [1989] for a discussion of this issue in relation to the treatment of borderline personality disorders.)

CONCLUSION

Both Mahler and Kohut have made seminal contributions to contemporary psychoanalytic theory and practice. To the extent that Mahler attempted to integrate her work into the paradigm of classical psychoanalytic theory and Kohut did not, many of the differences that exist between them may be noted or inferred in the "standard" critiques of self psychology (e.g., Curtis 1985, Kernberg 1974, Rothstein 1980, Treurniet 1980, Wallerstein 1983, 1985).

Despite the obvious disparities, however, Mahler and Kohut deserve comparative consideration, in that the work of each may be seen as a response to a series of tensions that have always existed in psychoanalytic theory and practice. These tensions assumed a position of greater prominence following the work of Hartmann (1939, 1964) and, as I have noted above, are still with us today. In their own way, Mahler and Kohut have each elaborated upon the vicissitudes of adaptation and the developmental point of view. They have contributed to our understanding of psychic regulation and homeostasis, self-esteem regulation, organization of the self, self cohesion, and object constancy.

Intrinsic to the work of each has been an appreciation of the roles played by reality and the real object relationship in normal and pathological development and in the treatment process. Their attention to aspects of the real relationship has encompassed a reexamination of the role of trauma and its consequences. This has been taken up in terms of the failure of the object to provide appropriate responses to the particular needs encountered during the subphases of the separation-individuation process (both originally and subsequently as their derivatives appear in the analytic situation) and in terms of empathic failure throughout development. In the therapeutic setting, both authors have made important contributions to our recognition of the way in which analysis recapitulates and may reinstitute previously arrested developmental trends. And each has contributed to the ongoing debate about the potential therapeutic role of the actual analytic interaction.

Finally, both Mahler and Kohut have made significant contributions to our beginning understanding of the pro-

cesses of internalization and the formation of psychic structure. Their descriptions of ego development and the trans-
formation of the structures of narcissism and self regulation
have illuminated the ways in which the processes of internalization derive from and depend upon actual object relationships as important way stations of environmental support for
the not yet—perhaps never fully—internalized psychic regulatory structures.

The views of Mahler and Kohut continue to challenge,
inform, and enrich our clinical technique, particularly as we
attempt to understand the subtle interactive dimensions of the
psychoanalytic process and the nature of the analyst's actual
participation in the analytic process. We remain indebted to
them as we continue to study, apply, and work out the
implications and consequences of their contributions, and
struggle with many of the same problems and issues, the
attempted solutions to which they have so richly endowed us.

REFERENCES

Adler, G. (1989). Uses and limitations of Kohut's self psychology in the treatment of
    borderline patients. *Journal of the American Psychoanalytic Association* 37:761–785.
Blum, H. (1971). Transference and structure. In *The Unconscious Today*, ed. M. Kanzer, pp.
    177–195. New York: International Universities Press.
Curtis, H. (1985). Clinical perspectives on self psychology. *Psychoanalytic Quarterly*
    54:339–378.
Fleming, J. (1972). Early object deprivation and transference phenomena: the working
    alliance. *Psychoanalytic Quarterly* 41:23–49.
—— (1975). Some observations on object constancy in the psychoanalysis of adults. *Journal
    of the American Psychoanalytic Association* 23:743–759.
Friedman, L. (1980). Kohut: a book review essay. *Psychoanalytic Quarterly* 49:393–422.
—— (1986). Kohut's testament. *Psychoanalytic Inquiry* 6:321–348.
Gitelson, M. (1962). The curative factors in psychoanalysis. I. The first phase of psychoanal-
    ysis. *International Journal of Psycho-Analysis* 43:194–205.
Greenacre P. (1975). On reconstruction. *Journal of the American Psychoanalytic Association*
    23:693–712.
Hartmann, H. (1939). *Ego Psychology and the Problem of Adaptation*. New York: International
    Universities Press, 1958.

_____ (1964). *Essays on Ego Psychology*. New York: International Universities Press.

Kernberg, O. (1974). Further contributions to the treatment of narcissistic personalities. *International Journal of Psycho-Analysis* 55:215–240.

Kohut, H. (1966). Forms and transformations of narcissism. *Journal of the American Psychoanalytic Association* 14:243–273.

_____ (1968). Psychoanalytic treatment of narcissistic personality disorders: outline of a systematic approach. *Psychoanalytic Study of the Child* 23:86–113. New York: International Universities Press.

_____ (1971). *The Analysis of the Self*. New York: International Universities Press.

_____ (1977). *The Restoration of the Self*. New York: International Universities Press.

_____ (1980). Reflection. In *Advances in Self Psychology*, ed. A. Goldberg, pp. 473–554. New York: International Universities Press.

_____ (1984). *How Does Analysis Cure?*, ed. A. Goldberg. Chicago: University of Chicago Press.

Kohut, H., and Wolf, E. (1978). The disorders of the self and their treatment: an outline. *International Journal of Psycho-Analysis* 59:413–425.

Kramer, S. (1979). The technical significance and application of Mahler's separation-individuation theory. *Journal of the American Psychoanalytic Association* 27(suppl): 241–262.

_____ (1990). Residues of incest. In *Adult Analysis and Childhood Sexual Abuse*, ed. H. B. Levine, pp. 149–170. Hillsdale, NJ: Analytic Press.

Kramer, S., and Akhtar, S. (1988). The developmental context of internalized preoedipal object relations: clinical applications of Mahler's theory of symbiosis and separation-individuation. *Psychoanalytic Quarterly* 57:547–576.

Levine, H. (1983). Some implications of self psychology. *Contemporary Psychoanalysis* 19:153–171.

_____ (1990). Introduction. In *Adult Analysis and Childhood Sexual Abuse*, ed. H. B. Levine, pp. 3–20. Hillsdale, NJ: Analytic Press.

Loewald, H. (1960). On the therapeutic action of psychoanalysis. *International Journal of Psycho-Analysis* 41:16–33.

Mahler, M. (1971). A study of the separation–individuation process and its possible application to borderline phenomena in the psychoanalytic situation. *The Psychoanalytic Study of the Child* 26:403–424. New Haven, CT: Yale University Press.

_____ (1979). *The Selected Papers of Margaret S. Mahler*. New York: Jason Aronson.

_____ (1988). *The Memoirs of Margaret S. Mahler*, compiled and edited by Paul E. Stepansky. New York and London: Free Press.

Mahler, M., Pine, F., and Bergman, A. (1975). *The Psychological Birth of the Human Infant: Symbiosis and Individuation*. New York: Basic Books.

Rothstein, A. (1980). Toward a critique of the psychology of the self. *Psychoanalytic Quarterly* 49:423–455.

Sandler, J. (1983). Reflections on some relations between psychoanalytic concepts and psychoanalytic practice. *International Journal of Psycho-Analysis* 64:35–46.

Settlage, C. (1977). The psychoanalytic understanding of narcissistic and borderline personality disorders: advances in developmental theory. *Journal of the American Psychoanalytic Association* 25:805–834.

—— (1989). The interplay of therapeutic and developmental process in the treatment of children: an application of contemporary object relations theory. *Psychoanalytic Inquiry* 9:375–396.

Shane, E., and Shane, M. (1989). Mahler, Kohut and infant research. Some comparisons. In *Self Psychology: Comparisons and Contrasts,* ed. D. W. Detrick and S. P. Detrick, pp. 395–413. Hillsdale, NJ: Analytic Press.

Stone, L. (1954). The widening scope of indications for psychoanalysis. *Journal of the American Psychoanalytic Association* 2:567–594.

Treurniet, N. (1980). On the relation between the concepts of self and ego in Kohut's psychology of the self. *International Journal of Psycho-Analysis* 61:325–333.

Wallerstein, R. (1983). Self psychology and "classical" psychoanalytic psychology: the nature of their relationship. *Psychoanalytic Contemporary Thought* 6:553–595.

—— (1985). How does self psychology differ in practice? *International Journal of Psycho-Analysis* 66:391–404.

—— (1988). One psychoanalysis or many? *International Journal of Psycho-Analysis* 69:5–22.

Zetzel, E. (1965). The theory of therapy in relation to a developmental model of the psychic apparatus. *International Journal of Psycho-Analysis* 46:39–52.

7

Contrasting Roles of Narcissistic Mirroring in Self Psychology and Separation-Individuation Theory

Discussion of Levine's Chapter "Mahler and Kohut: A Comparative View"

Thomas Wolman, M.D.

I am pleased to have the opportunity to discuss Dr. Levine's thoughtful and stimulating chapter. He has done an admirable job of bringing together the common elements in the work of Mahler and Kohut, while at the same time exploring the tensions and strains that divide them in theory and practice. The comparison between these two seminal thinkers is useful in highlighting the tensions and interrelationships between *deficit* and *conflict* in contemporary psychoanalytic thinking. And as Levine notes in his chapter, it also demonstrates the impossibility of creating a complete theoretical synthesis. I came to the same conclusion while writing a paper comparing Mahler and Winnicott (Wolman 1991). Mahler and Winnicott are, if anything, closer together on a number of issues than are Mahler and Kohut. This is necessarily true because Winnicott influenced Mahler's work *in statu nascendi*, as it were. And yet even two thinkers as intellectually compatible as Mahler and Winnicott revealed many strains and divergencies. I believe

these strains have as much to teach us as the points of confluence—perhaps more.

The common ground between Mahler and Kohut includes the importance of empathy, the role of real object
relationships, the impact of early environmental failure, and
the viewpoint that analysis embodies a developmental process. Each of these ideas is a whole topic in itself, and could
easily be the subject of a chapter. I have therefore chosen to
limit my discussion to one striking similarity in the work of
Mahler and Kohut—the phenomenon of *mirroring identification,* which they apparently discovered independently of each
other. Perhaps Kohut (1980) had mirroring in mind when he
said that he and Mahler were "digging tunnels from different
directions into the same area of the mountain." However, I
think the two tunnels continue past the point of confluence,
conveying Mahler and Kohut to different sides of the mountain. In this regard, I hope to extend Dr. Levine's argument
that, despite their similarities, Mahler and Kohut reach different conclusions on the role of mirroring in later development and in psychoanalytic practice.

MIRRORING IDENTIFICATION

In her observational work, Mahler and colleagues (1975) gave
detailed descriptions of *mirroring* between mother and child
and explored its functions for the developing psyche. Mirroring appeared in the context of the mutual "matching" and
accommodation between mother and child that characterizes
the symbiotic phase. The earliest mirroring could be found in
the infant's first attempts to "mold" itself to the mother's
body. However, Mahler and colleagues (1975) maintained
that the eye to eye contact with the mother, and particularly
the visual fixation on her face, was essential for the full
development of symbiosis. Later, such visual fixation was

extended to family members such as siblings, the peer group, and the reflection in an actual mirror.

Mahler viewed mirroring as an important—perhaps the essential—aspect of symbiosis. The sense of dual unity between mother and child is perhaps nowhere more apparent than in the moment when the child sees herself in the gleam of her mother's eye, the moment when she sees herself being seen, as it were. The sharing of the gaze is almost like a *tether*—in Akhtar's (1991) use of the term—that maintains symbiotic attachment. The eye to eye contact then becomes the basis of an ongoing "dialogue" of mutual cuing and reciprocal exchange of facial gestures. In all her descriptions, Mahler emphasizes the triad of eye contact, reciprocity or mutuality, and nonverbal communication.

Kohut (1971) speaks of the infantile origin of *mirroring transferences* in very similar terms. He defines the principal mirror transference as

> the therapeutic reinstatement of that normal phase of the development of the grandiose self in which the gleam in the mother's eye, which mirrors the child's exhibitionistic display, and other forms of maternal participation in and response to the child's narcissistic-exhibitionistic enjoyment confirm the child's self-esteem and, by a gradually increasing selectivity of these responses, begin to channel it into realistic directions. [p. 116]

This definition emphasizes the visual modality, a fact that Kohut acknowledges in a reference to the special problems of blind children in establishing a mirroring relationship.

According to Kohut, the function of mirroring is the establishment of a cohesive self. He describes this achievement (1971) as "the growth of self experience as a physical and mental unit which has cohesiveness in space and continuity in time" (p. 118). For the first time, the child sees himself as a whole person in his mother's eyes, whereas before, he saw himself as nothing but a bundle of body parts. The newly acquired ego integration enhances the child's capacity for work and play, and the new narcissistic libidinal cathexis of the self promotes well-being and raises self-esteem. However, when maternal mirroring has been insufficient, the unity of the self remains precarious and tends to dissolve during regressive states.

Mahler also stressed the importance of early mirroring for the integration of the body image. On this subject she quotes Greenacre (1960) as follows:

> Vision is not only an adjunct but an indispensable one in establishing the confluence of the body surface and promoting awareness of delimitation of the self from non-self. "Touching" and taking in of the various body parts with the eyes (vision) helps in drawing the body together, into a central image beyond the level of mere immediate sensory awareness. [p. 208]

Mahler and Kohut also agree that mirroring is essential for the narcissistic investment of the self and the consequent regulation of self-esteem. The mother's loving affirmation of her child is reflected in her face and continually amplified in the ongoing "dialogue" with her child. Mahler discovered normal cyclothymic mood swings in the child in response to the stability and variability of maternal mirroring. During the mother's brief absence, some children underwent a period of "low-keyedness" that Mahler and colleagues (1975) speculated may be akin to a "miniature anaclitic depression." At the other pole, during the practicing subphase, narcissism is at its peak, and the child enjoys a love affair with the world. A part of the elation felt after the mastery of upright locomotion may derive from the child's mirroring identification with the, to him or her, awesomely grand stature of the parents. Mahler and colleagues (1975) say, in this regard, that the "upright posture brings a sense of exhilaration, as if the child had already graduated into the world of independent human beings" (p. 74).

Descriptions of mirroring elsewhere in the world psychoanalytic literature show striking concordance with Mahler and Kohut's views, and hence add to the credibility of the phenomenon. References to mirroring go back to Freud (1920) himself, who described a mirror game played by his 18-month-old grandson. In 1949, the French analyst, Jacques Lacan, presented a paper at the International Psychoanalytic Congress at Zurich, titled "The Mirror Stage as Formative of the Function of the I as Revealed in Psychoanalytic Experience."

Partly influenced by that paper, Winnicott (1971) discussed mirroring in a paper titled "Mirror-role of Mother and Family in Child Development." The basic tenet of this paper is that "the precursor of the mirror is the mother's face" (p. 130). Hence, when the baby looks into the mother's face, what he sees is himself, or rather his emotional *effect* on the mother reflected in her face. Besides acknowledging its narcissistic value for the child, Winnicott stressed the role of mirroring in stimulating the child's imaginative capacity. According to Winnicott, the mirroring relationship with the mother lays the foundation for a creative interchange with reality, in which perception becomes apperception, "a two-way process in which self-enrichment alternates with the discovery of meaning in the world of seen things" (p. 132).

Winnicott was also among the first to postulate that failures of the mirroring relationship have grave emotional consequences. These include atrophy of the imaginative capacity and emotional withdrawal from a mother who is perceived as an inert object. Winnicott also thought that partial failure of maternal mirroring produced defensive reactions, such as exaggerated wooing behavior and a tendency to scan the mother's face for signs of interest. He predicted that such a child would not grasp the function of an actual mirror. As he put it, the mirroring–deprived child would view the mirror as a thing "to be looked at" rather than a thing "to be looked into" (p. 132).

Mahler confirmed many of Winnicott's conjectures in her observations of mothers and their children. She detailed numerous correlations between mirroring behavior, mood disturbances, and separation from the mother (Mahler et al. 1975). One child, who was separated from his mother while he was in the hospital, and then again after the birth of a baby brother, began to take a great interest in his image in the mirror. In addition, he was observed to make "mirror identifications" with his older siblings and with other school-age children. Mahler speculated that this exaggerated mirroring helped to defend against feelings of depression. Another child, who seemed especially sensitive to brief separations from the mother, developed a precocious mirroring identification with the mother at age 7 months.

Mahler and her co-workers' observations of one particular child, Teddy, are especially revealing. Teddy had been denied visual access to his mother's face when he was a young infant. He had compensated, in part with the encouragement of his mother, by forming a kind of twinship with his brother Charlie. However, he still showed a lag in the integration of his body image in his third year. When shown a photograph of himself and asked "Where's Teddy?" he would point only to his eyes, nose, and mouth, rather than to his whole body. This would correspond to Kohut's descriptions of the failure to achieve a cohesive self.

Mahler's findings are at least consistent with the hypothesis that a disturbance in the mirroring relationship with the mother, most often caused by her absence, can give rise to an exaggerated, compensatory mirroring with others. Mahler seems to favor the notion that such mirroring compensates for disturbances in the self-image, and that it may function as a defense against depression. Thus her findings lend some weight to Kohut's idea that "empathic failure" in early life leads to the development of mirror transferences.

One reason separation–individuation theory did not become a self psychology is its insistence on exploring the self in connection with correlative agencies such as self-image, body schema, body ego, ideal ego, ego ideal, and superego. The self is never equated with the psyche as a whole. Indeed, Mahler and colleagues (1975) show that unconscious forces play a major role in influencing the mirroring phenomenon, imparting various degrees of distortion. One child, for example, unconsciously conformed to the mother's unconscious demand that she stand erect on the mother's lap. Mahler found that this position, which grossly inhibited the child's freedom of movement, became highly libidinized and preferred by the young infant. In a footnote, she correlates her observation to Greenacre's (1959) suggestion that the child's body represents a penis in the mother's unconscious. This example is important because it demonstrates the element of illusion in mirroring identification. What the child sees as a complete picture of herself is in fact only a partial one at best.

Kohut seems at times to accept the self revealed in mirroring at face value. In his thinking, the self gradually acquires an independent life of its own, and eventually takes over the territory occupied by the psyche. Hence, Kohut tends to see mirroring as inherently growth producing regardless of the stage of development in which it takes place, or of the other interagency conflicts that might be impinging upon it. The logic of this position then demands that psychopathology be viewed always in terms of *empathic failure*, for which read "the absence of mirroring." For Mahler, on the other hand, inadequate mirroring is only one of many factors having an impact on the process of separation–individuation.

THE FATE OF MIRRORING IN THE
SEPARATION-INDIVIDUATION PROCESS

Thus, despite their remarkable confluence of thought on the subject of the mirroring phenomenon, Mahler and Kohut part ways on the significance of mirroring for future development. For Kohut, as I understand him, mirroring is the main prototype for future development, and the main cure for early environmental failure. Levine highlights these conclusions in his chapter. He quotes Kohut as saying, "It is the empathic bond and its continual repair by empathic understanding that does the curing" (Friedman 1986, p. 327). "A successful analysis is one in which the analysand's formerly archaic needs for the responses of archaic selfobjects are superseded by the experience of the availability of empathic resonance, the major constituent of the sense of security in adult life" (Kohut 1984, p. 77).

Indeed, for Kohut, mirroring is synonymous with the very notion of object relationship. The concept of selfobject implies that no object is entirely separated from the self, since the one is always capable of mirroring some aspect of the other. Thus, Kohut tends to view development in the narrow sense of a developmental line leading from archaic selfobject relationships to "the availability of empathic resonance" in adult life. His view places less emphasis upon internalization and the attainment of autonomy, and more on the mature and resourceful use of others as mirroring alter egos. In this area, Kohut's thinking reminds us that exernal objects can replace intrapsychic functions even in adult life—witness for example Freud's (1921) group psychology—and that object constancy is never fully achieved (Mahler et al. 1975).

For Mahler, however, the primary fate of early mirroring is to be disrupted, mourned, and replaced by other more symbolic relational modalities. She views the onset of the rapprochement phase as a disruption of the old mirroring, of the stage of preverbal empathy. At the age of 18 to 21 months, the child arrives at the anxious realization of his own limited powers and the loss of his or her omnipotence. Most importantly, the illusion (or delusion in Mahler's words) of dual unity is lost when the child realizes that he and his mother are not of one mind, that their wishes do not always coincide, and that their empathy is no longer perfect, if indeed it ever was (Mahler et al. 1975).

Interestingly, Mahler et al. (1975) noted a change in the reaction to mirrors and in the quality of identifications. Children with severe, lingering, stranger anxiety feel frightened when they see themselves in the mirror, almost as if their own image were strange to them. It would appear they are distressed by this reminder of their own separation. The healthy older toddler no longer confuses himself with his mirror image. Observed looking in the mirror, he appears to be trying to distinguish himself from his mirror image, that is, to be using the mirror to establish his separateness. The ability to recognize one's mirror image is further enhanced by the use of the word *I*.

Mahler details with great clarity the child's sometimes almost desperate efforts to reinstate the old preverbal modality, despite the growing awareness of his own separateness. Several of the rapprochement phase specific behaviors seem designed to coerce the mother into a more regressive, mirroring relationship with her child. In "shadowing," for example, the child watches the mother incessantly, following her every move, as if the two were inseparable again. "Darting away" appears to express the opposite tendency— namely, the fear of engulfment—but may also provoke the mother's pursuit. Mahler also speaks of the child's "coercive gestures" and "wooing" as further attempts to reestablish dual unity by using the mother as an extension of the self. Typically, the child would expect "that mother, summoned by some magical gesture alone, rather than with words, would guess and fulfill the toddler's momentary wish" (Mahler et al. 1975, p. 95).

Many of these examples seem like a last ditch effort to communicate in gestures rather than via the emerging capacity for verbalized speech. Mahler recognized this resistance to verbalization as one aspect of the ongoing struggle to work through the rapprochement crisis. The ambivalence over saying things in words comes from their power to separate. In this regard, Mahler drew attention to words like *cookie,* which the toddler uses to articulate the wish "I want a cookie." Ironically, such advances in communication help to disrupt the illusion of omnipotence and dual unity. The requirement of having to say what you want implies that the mother does not know what you want or does not always want what you want at the moment that you want it.

However, once begun, verbalized speech becomes the main technique for resolving the rapprochement crisis and the main avenue for the achievement of separation. The mourning for the lost omnipotence is mainly worked through in the area of symbolized play, and with the help of transitional objects. The process is enhanced by transitional activities like the reading of stories that stimulate symbolic play. Mahler and colleagues (1975) also stress the child's ability to name objects, to verbalize wishes, and especially to use the word *I* to refer to him- or herself. Understanding of verbalized speech also makes possible higher-level internalization of rules, demands, and other symbolic aspects of parenting.

These higher-level symbolic activities point the way toward the castration and Oedipus complexes. Indeed, Mahler implicitly saw rapprochement as a kind of preparation and prototype for the Oedipus. Verbalization, for example, constitutes the first breach in the illusion of dual unity, hence a sort of precursor to the incest barrier. Simultaneous with this development is the growing importance of the father as a love object for the child. Mahler and colleagues (1975) state that "although he is not fully outside the symbiotic union, neither is he ever fully part of it" (p. 91). Moreover, the child very early perceives a special relationship between the parents, which by implication (an implication realized at a later date) does not include him. The introduction of an object placed *outside* of the original twosome produces a rudimentary triangularity.

The correlation of rapprochement with the child's discovery of the anatomical sexual difference indicates a profound link with the castration complex. Mahler and colleagues (1975) found the emotional consequences of this discovery to be most pronounced in little girls. The little girl's somewhat premature discovery of sex difference aroused intense anxiety, anger, and defiance—in short, an exacerbation of the rapprochement crisis. Within the context of rapprochement issues, one might say that the narcissistic injury of not having a penis is experienced by some little girls as a breach in the mirroring relationship with the mother. The feeling of "lacking something" is incompatible with the plenitude of dual unity.

One gets the impression from reading Mahler that most boys do not fully come to grips with the anatomical sex difference until the oedipal period at ages 4 to 6. But for the boy as well, the working out of the castration complex also involves the loss or modification of the mirroring relationship with the mother. The boy's phallic phase is marked by a return of narcissistic mirroring. Little Hans (Freud 1909), for example, loved to look at other people's genitals, especially his mother's, to see how they compared with his own. His theory that everyone possesses a penis reflected his powerful mirroring identification with the entire object world. The ensuing struggles over the reality of castration forced him to modify his "weltanschauung" and to replace mirroring with symbolic processes.

This digression on the third subphase of separation-individuation is meant to highlight Mahler and Kohut's very different views on the fate of mirroring in human development. Mahler sees mirroring as an essential precursor to the separation–individuation process, which, however, must be partly dissolved and substantially modified. The gradual dissolution of mirroring begins in the rapprochement phase and continues in the oedipal phase. In Mahler's developmental viewpoint, rapprochement is intimately linked with the Oedipus insofar as it prefigures many of the tasks and conflicts of the latter phase and also its means of resolution through mourning (Freud 1924) and symbolic processes.

It seems to me that Kohut does not put quite so much stress on the importance of separation, on the disruption of mirroring, or on the critical role of verbalized speech. He continues to see development as a restoration of a previous state of affairs rather than as a reconciliation with new realities. While Mahler views both rapprochement and the Oedipus as unavoidable impasses in development, Kohut conceives of them as pathological only when mirroring in the broad sense is not reciprocated by the parents. In this sense, his outlook tends more toward the romantic, while Mahler is a bit closer to Freud's sense of the tragic, defined as the inevitability of loss and change.

This difference in outlook and emphasis is reflected in Kohut's view of the process of verbalization and interpretation in analysis. For Kohut (1984), the primary function of the analyst's verbalized understanding is not to promote separation but to facilitate an "identity of inner experiences" (p. 184). While such identity may be lessened during the phase of analysis he calls "explanation," it is still "empathic understanding" that does the curing. As cited in Dr. Levine's chapter, "Explanation . . . is useful mainly because it helps to sustain (and demonstrate to the patient) the empathic bond" (Friedman 1986, p. 327). By contrast, Mahler always main-

tained that verbalization was critical to the achievement of separation, and by extension to the psychoanalytic process.

IMPLICATIONS FOR PSYCHOANALYTIC TECHNIQUE

Historically speaking, Freud (1913) was the first to consider the technical implications of mirroring in his formulation of the psychoanalytic method. Early on, he adopted the plan of "getting the patient to lie on a sofa while I sit behind him out of his sight" (p.133). He admitted that the arrangement was partly due to a personal motive, namely a dislike of being stared at for eight hours a day. However, he also realized that constant eye contact with the patient would have made it impossible for him to freely give himself over to the current of his unconscious thoughts. Nor did he want his facial expressions to supply feedback about his internal states to the patient, thus influencing the development of the transference. Hence, mirroring was excluded from psychoanalysis very origin.

Much of the atmosphere in which analysis is conducted with its stress on the analyst's relative neutrality and ity, can be traced back to the barrier against mirroring example, Freud (1912) writes:

Young and eager psycho-analysts will no doubt be bring their own individuality freely into the order to carry the patient along with them and barriers of his own narrow personality. It m that it would be quite allowable and indeed to overcoming the patient's existing resista and, by giving him intimate informatic

enable him to put himself on an equal footing. One confidence deserves another, and anyone who demands intimacy from someone else must be prepared to give it in return. [p. 117]

In this quotation, Freud wants to distance himself from any therapy based upon narcissistic mirroring. The tendency for the analyst to show his own personality is another way of showing his "face." The idea would be to encourage and elicit a mirror reaction in the patient, thus establishing an exact analogue of the early mirroring relationship between mother and child. The disadvantages of this technique, according to Freud, are virtually the same as those resulting from regular eye contact with the patient, namely a subsequent increase in resistance, a contamination of the transference, and especially a block to uncovering what is unconscious in the patient. Freud's recommendation that analysts be *opaque* to their patients amounts, in effect, to a prohibition against mutual narcissistic mirroring.

This Freudian background helps to place in perspective the divergence between Mahler and Kohut in the area of psychoanalytic technique. The essence of this difference in technique is contained in a quotation from Dr. Levine's chapter:

The therapist must avoid the pitfall of indefinitely accepting the patient's transference expectation for purposes of meeting an early object need. Such a compensatory supply has value in the beginning, but indefinite acceptance fails to help the patient differentiate the past from the present and can reinforce the state of arrested development in the ego and self-system. [Fleming 1972, p. 44]

In other words, the therapist must go beyond mere mirroring in order to facilitate the development of an analytic process. From the point of view of the therapist, this change is

indicated by Mahler's choice of the term *emotional availability,* which may continue even in the absence of mutual empathy. As is now well known, Mahler and colleagues (1975) studied the mother's confused reaction to her rapprochement-phase youngster's contradictory behavior. The mother's reactions were often "tinged with annoyance"—probably an under-statement—at her child's abrupt changeover from excessive clinging to pushing her away. But even when she felt out of touch with her child, she usually remained emotionally avail-able and capable of "containing" the emotions that were being stirred up within her.

The "emotional fine-tuning" example from Dr. Kra-mer's paper (1979), quoted by Levine, applies this attitude to the analytic situation. She notes that "the analyst had to be available but had to be careful not to 'shadow'" (p. 251). In other words, being available is consistent with not playing in to the mirroring that the patient seems to expect. A space of separation has to be opened up where transference enactments can be verbalized and symbolically worked over in the ana-lytic process. The other example of a technique drawn from Fleming (1975) demonstrates just how the absence of the analyst, that is, the loss of mirroring identification, can be compensated by the symbolic and transitional activity of free associating and reporting the results to her (the analyst) in their subsequent sessions.

On the other hand, these technical suggestions at least raise the issue of those patients for whom loss of eye contact with the analyst represents an extreme privation. Akhtar (1991) has discussed the move from chair to couch as a potential disruption of the "optimal distance" between anal-ysis and patient. Mahony (1989) and Almansi (1979) have written about patients who exhibit a compulsive need to look at the analyst's face. Although this behavior was analyzed, the treatment still required some periods when eye contact was maintained. Both Mahony and Almansi held that such "looking" originated during early separation-individuation, and reflected a disturbance in early narcissistic mirroring. For these patients, the loss of eye contact with the analyst may represent a repetition in the present of an infantile trauma. The question then becomes: Are these patients capable of analyzing their craving to see the analyst while immersed in a situation that replicates certain aspects of the original trauma? Perhaps such patients could make better use of analysis, at least initially, within a Kohutian framework.

CONCLUSION

These reflections bring to mind a case vignette of my own, with which I would like to conclude my discussion. I used to see a graduate student in his mid-twenties in face to face psychotherapy. Given the schizoid and alexithymic qualities of his personality, the regular eye contact was helpful in providing an initial approach to the transference. This patient was acutely sensitive to body language and facial expressions. There were times when he would ask me to keep my body absolutely still because he experienced my movements as a mirroring of his own anxiety. The transference was initially drawn on very primitive lines, involving our sharing various bodily organs. However, at the very least, this mirroring served to anchor the transference, providing it with a point of attachment and a framework on which to work out separation issues.

These came to the fore quite early when he began to complain bitterly about my lack of empathy. We were just never on the same wavelength, as far as he was concerned. How could I help him if I could never truly understand what it felt like to be him? Then one day he said something especially revealing about himself. He said, "You know I can't stand the fact that I have to tell you things, that I have to go through the awkward, painful process of putting things into words. I wish to God you would just know about these things before I had to say them, so you could respond without my having to say them."

In retrospect, I believe this relative failure of mirroring, in the context of an initial phase of mirroring identification—in essence a reenactment of rapprochement-phase issues—helped this patient initiate a process of separation-individuation.

REFERENCES

Akhtar, S. (1991). *Tethers, orbits, and invisible fences: clinical, developmental, and sociocultural aspects of optimal distance.* Paper presented at the 22nd annual Margaret S. Mahler Symposium on Child Development.

Almansi, R. (1979). Scopophilia and object loss. *Psychoanalytic Quarterly* 48:601–619.

Fleming, J. (1972). Early object deprivation and transference phenomena: the working alliance. *Psychoanalytic Quarterly* 41:23–49.

_____ (1975). Some observations on object constancy in the psychoanalysis of adults. *Journal of the American Psychoanalytic Association* 23:743–759.

Friedman, L. (1986). Kohut's testament. *Psychoanalytic Inquiry* 6:321–348.

Freud, S. (1909). Analysis of a phobia in a five-year-old boy. *Standard Edition* 10:3–150.

_____ (1912). Recommendations to physicians practising psychoanalysis. *Standard Edition* 12:109–121.

_____ (1913). On beginning the treatment (further recommendations on the technique of psychoanalysis I). *Standard Edition* 12:121–145.

_____ (1920). Beyond the pleasure principle. *Standard Edition* 18:7–64.

_____ (1921). Group psychology and the analysis of the ego. *Standard Edition* 18:7–64.

_____ (1924). The dissolution of the Oedipus complex. *Standard Edition* 20:77–174.

Greenacre, P. (1959). On focal symbiosis. In *Dynamic Psychology in Childhood*, ed. L. Jessner and E. Pavenstedt, pp. 243–256. New York: Grune & Stratton.

_____ (1960). Considerations regarding the parent–infant relationship. In *Emotional Growth*, vol. 1, pp. 199–224. New York: International Universities Press.

Kohut, H. (1971). *The Analysis of the Self.* New York: International Universities Press.

_____ (1980). Reflection. In *Advances in Self Psychology*, ed. A. Goldberg, pp. 473–554. New York: International Universities Press.

_____ (1984). *How Does Analysis Cure?*, ed. A. Goldberg. Chicago: University of Chicago Press.

Kramer, S. (1979). The technical significance and application of Mahler's separation-individuation theory. *Journal of the American Psychoanalytic Association* 27(suppl): 241–262.

Lacan, J. (1949). The mirror stage as formative of the function of the I as revealed in psychoanalytic experience. In *Ecrits,* pp. 1–7. New York: W. W. Norton, 1977.

Mahler, M., Pine, F., and Bergman, A. (1975). *The Psychological Birth of the Human Infant: Symbiosis and Individuation.* New York: Basic Books.

Mahony, P. J. (1989). Aspects of nonperverse scopophilia within an analysis. *Journal of the American Psychoanalytic Association* 37:365–401.

Winnicott, D. W. (1971). *Playing and Reality.* New York: Penguin Books.

Wolman, T. (1991). Mahler and Winnicott: some parallels in their lives and works. In *Beyond the Symbiotic Orbit: Advances in Separation-Individuation Theory. Essays in Honor of Selma Kramer, M.D.,* ed. S. Akhtar and H. Parens, pp. 35–60. Hillsdale, NJ: Analytic Press.

8

An Interactional View of Development, Pathogenesis, and Therapeutic Process: Complexity and Hazards

Concluding Reflections on Settlage's, Wolf's, and Levine's Chapters

Newell Fischer, M.D.

In reflecting on so much rich and varied material, and in an effort to keep this chapter brief and focused, I have elected to underscore and comment on just one theme that ran through the three principal chapters and that attracted my attention. Clearly such selective attention, or inattention, does not do justice to the rich array of material that has been presented, but it might be preferable to be so focused.

In the brief history of psychoanalysis, there has been a variety of pendular shifts in how we think about the mind and how we understand the things we experience and the kinds of phenomena we allow ourselves to observe. Dr. Levine has alluded to this when he suggested that our psychoanalytic focus has moved from the outer world of events to intrapsychic phenomena and more recently back to the world around us—real objects and actual object relationships.

Freud's early seduction theory yielded, through his self-analysis, discoveries of the inner world and unconscious fantasy. Dr. Levine points out, following this new introspective view, this new horizon to be explored, there was an "urgent, even exuberant, rush to elaborate upon the implications of psychic reality and the vicissitudes of instinctual development" and perhaps an underemphasis and neglect of the roles of actual experience and the real object. In the late 1930s, with the growth of ego psychology and Hartmann's emphasis on adaptation, we witnessed a swing back to a greater appreciation of the surround, an appreciation that became part of the backdrop for the studies of Kohut and Mahler.

It is noteworthy that one sees a similar shift in the current focus in general psychiatric practice. In recent years there has been great interest in and indeed even a preoccupation with "historical" truth and in discovering the "real" events of childhood. Clinical reports related to dissociative disorders and posttraumatic stress disorders, syndromes often related to traumatic life events, abound and appear to be multiplying. Psychiatrists-in-training as well as experienced clinicians often see themselves as detectives, bent on uncovering deep family secrets. Patients in emotional distress and caught up in early transferential pulls, may be very obliging and quite suggestive to this kind of exploration.

The element that stood out for me as I read the previous chapters, the element I would like to underscore, is the emphasis placed on the interactional factors shaping developmental unfolding and psychopathogenesis. This interactional focus also very much guides the authors' understanding of the nature of the therapeutic process—that is, what in the psychoanalytic encounter stimulates growth and change.

THE INTERACTIONAL FOCUS

In my comments about the interactional theme that I see running through the chapters, I will concentrate on two areas: (1) the nature and complexity of this interaction, and (2) how the focus and emphasis on the interactional elements have the potential of drawing us away from understanding and addressing the intrapsychic domain of our work as psychoanalysts.

The earlier chapters clearly underscore the mutuality and complexity of the interaction between the parents and the child in the developmental context, and of the interplay between analyst and analysand in the therapeutic encounter. In discussing the developmental unfolding of the infant, Wolf emphasizes the neonate's predictable need for psychological experiences, especially for attuned responsiveness from caregivers. In keeping with current infant observational research, Wolf and self psychologists generally hypothesize a psychological give-and-take interaction that is needed for psychic growth. In citing a variety of developmental studies, Wolf notes the mutual regulation between caregiver and child. The central concept of selfobject responses, intrinsic to the self psychological perspective, encompasses both the complexities and interplay between infant and his surround as well as the psychological connection between patient and analyst. Wolf notes the need for selfobject responses that is always present, "waxing and waning with the ups and downs of the strength and vulnerability of the self," and is an inevitable part of the transference–countertransference engagement in the analytic relationship. Wolf elaborates, "The analysand's unconscious and the analyst's unconscious surely influence each other to an extent that is unknowable by either. . . . [A] therapeutic process rests on what happens between analysand and analyst, expecially on the subjective feeling states of each in response to each other."

In a related fashion, Settlage acknowledges and underscores the complexities of the interactional element in developmental unfolding, in pathogenesis, and in the therapeutic process. As Settlage extrapolates from his research on the appeal cycle in children to the dynamics of the therapeutic encounter, the importance of the mutual interplay between the two participants becomes a principal element. The child reaching out to the parent, and the patient seeking some contact with the analyst, are relationships ideally character- ized by empathic and emotional availability and responsivity. Settlage states, "The patient's experience of the analyst's qual- ities as a human being is an essential part of the therapeutic and developmental processes."

I have elected to briefly underscore Drs. Wolf and Sett- lage's descriptions of the rich and complex and mutually interactive elements in human development and in the thera- peutic endeavor, because I see this as a particularly valuable contribution to our discussion. In the recent past, simpler and less sophisticated models have dominated our literature (Po- lansky et al. 1981, Rosen 1953, Saul 1980) and at times such perspectives appear to linger in our clinical thinking. A uni- directional and reductionistic model of the dyadic relationship may seriously diminish and skew our understanding of human interactions. Judd Marmor (1983) suggested that in efforts to study the etiology of human psychopathology, our appreciation can be grossly distorted and lead to fallacious or simplistic conclusions if a reductionistic set of premises guides our thinking. He noted that in using these reductionistic approaches clinicians "all share a tendency to think of causa- tion in linear, unifactorial terms, rather than in terms of the complex pluralistic, multifactorial dynamics that are involved in all human psychopathology" (p. 835).

In reviewing the literature for a paper I wrote in 1986 entitled "Witch Hunting: A Form of Reductionistic Think- ing" (Fischer 1986), I was impressed by the number of studies based on such simplistic models. This was most vividly seen in the many references concerning the "schizophrenogenic mother" (Arieti 1955, Lidz and Fleck 1960). In the more reductionistic paradigms, the infant's personality and psyche are seen as formless malleable clay, to be shaped by the actions and attitudes of the caregiver. More recent studies of neonatal and child development have highlighted the complex interplay between infant and mother. The data underscoring the profound influence the infant has on the caregiver is abundant and quite convincing (Emde 1980, Lichtenberg 1983, Papousek and Papousek 1983, Shapiro and Stern 1980, Stern 1985).

In a corresponding fashion, using a simplistic model in viewing the treatment setting, the patient is seen as being affected, altered, and influenced in a unidirectional manner by the powerful therapist. Such a perspective is contrary to our increasing appreciation in the past decade of countertransference phenomena, the transference–countertransference interface, identification processes, and so forth. Our understanding of the role of the patient in the therapeutic encounter and the multileveled and complex aspect of this interactive relationship has deepened considerably. A fine example of this is seen in Betty Joseph's papers of the late 1980s wherein she addresses these complex issues with eloquence when she discusses projective identification and the therapeutic process (Joseph 1989; also see Casement 1990 and Jacobs 1986).

Drs. Wolf and Settlage address the complexities inherent in the dyadic relationship when they emphasize the interactional component of development, psychopathogenesis, and therapeutic action. This emphasis is an important contribution.

My second point may at first glance seem a contradiction of my previous remarks. Whereas I have noted and applauded the earlier chapters' demonstration of the rich and complex nature of the interactional elements in development, pathogenesis, and therapeutic action, I am concerned, however, that the emphasis they place on this interactional component may obscure an important, indeed defining, aspect of our work as psychoanalysts. Further elaboration is in order.

Dr. Levine in his chapter outlined in broad strokes some

of the similarities and differences in views held by Mahler and Kohut. He then underscored the fact that "Intrinsic to the work of each [Mahler and Kohut] has been an appreciation of the roles played by reality and the real object relationship in normal and pathological development and in the treatment process." He further notes that Mahler and Kohut have contributed to our understanding of the "subtle interactive dimensions of the psychoanalytic process and the nature of the analyst's actual participation in the analytic process."

Drs. Wolf and Settlage in their chapters start from the general theories of Kohut and Mahler and add their own unique contributions. Both Drs. Wolf and Settlage have divided their chapters into three sections: (1) a review and elaboration of normal development as outlined by Kohut and Mahler, (2) a perspective on the process of psychopathogenesis, and (3) a view of the therapeutic process that grows out of their formulations about development and pathogenesis. As I read these chapters, I was again impressed by the fact that Drs. Wolf and Settlage have emphasized the interactional and the interpersonal facet of developmental unfolding and psychopathogenesis. In so doing I believe they have set the stage for a particular view of therapeutic intervention and a particular understanding of therapeutic action.

Dr. Wolf in discussing the developmental needs of infants and the needs of adults, emphasizes the requirements for "certain kinds of inputs from objects to achieve and maintain the self's cohesion, boundaries, vitality, and balance." These selfobject experiences, which very specifically emphasize interactional dynamics, include such experiential needs as mirroring, idealization, alter ego, ally–antagonist, efficacy, and vitalization of affects. This interplay between caregiver and infant is crucial in the development of the self and remains essential in some form and to some degree throughout the life cycle. When such selfobject experiences are defective or absent, Dr. Wolf and self psychologists suggest that there emerge various forms of psychological dysfunction ranging from mild levels of distress to frank psychosis. Kohut's theory and Wolf's elaboration clearly focus on the interactional and on the transaction between the individual and his surround.

Dr. Settlage underscores the interactional aspect of the separation–individuation process as proposed by Mahler. This is particularly evident when he describes his research on the appeal cycle—a reflection of the rapprochement subphase. Settlage skillfully outlines aspects of the separation–individuation theory, noting "the innately programmed thrust of individuation as a major motivation of development." He states that the developmental steps in the separation–individuation process introduce a series of minimal losses of mutual involvement to the child and the parent and that these successive losses are emotionally painful and sometimes resisted by the infant or/and the parent. In moving on to the realm of psychopathogenesis, Dr. Settlage indicates that the interaction between infant and caregiver is central and states that his "understanding of preoedipal pathogenesis is derived from the interactional model of development." Becoming even more specific, Settlage enumerates various ways that parents can interfere with the separation–individuation process, including (1) a failure to encourage and sanction separation–individuation, (2) the parent's inability to assuage and regulate the child's angry feelings and reestablish a viable developmental relationship, and (3) the parent's excessive need to control the child. Dr. Settlage then enumerates a variety of ways the child might defend against or adaptively respond to this parental interference. The appeal cycle that Dr. Settlage describes is a fascinating study of the interplay between the mother and child of the rapprochement subphase.

So, as with Dr. Wolf's discussion and Dr. Levine's comparative overview, we see in Dr. Settlage's chapter a focus on the interactional, the interpersonal, the real objects; on the dance that goes on between mother and infant; on actual flaws and impediments in this interplay; and on residuals, arrests, and derailments in these processes that may subsequently manifest themselves in a variety of forms of psychological dysfunction.

A DIFFERENT VANTAGE POINT

I have underscored, perhaps even exaggerated, the interactional focus of these chapters in an effort to contrast it to a different vantage point, a different aspect or a different way of thinking about developmental unfolding and psychic life. I refer to a focus that more specifically addresses the inner world of the child. As I read these chapters, I found my thinking shifting further and further away from the inner life of the children and adults being described. The inner world of wishes, fantasies, intrapsychic conflict, sources of anxiety, and inner struggles seems to pale, move to the background, and give way to a dynamic picture of who did what to whom, or how in tune was the caregiver with the infant. It should be clearly stated that these two perspectives—the interactional and the intrapsychic—by no means contradict each other. Indeed, one might say these views complement each other; they organize the data at different levels of abstraction. However, as one reads these chapters, it appears as if the interactional perspective has eclipsed our view and our interest in the inner world of the developing child and the symptomatic adult. My concern comes in how this balance or emphasis then becomes translated in the therapeutic arena, that is, how we see what it is we do and how we see what is therapeutic in what we do.

What helps people psychotherapeutically, what ingredients of the therapeutic process resolve conflict and free up the processes of growth are issues that are less than clear. I sense that the more we put the process of psychoanalytic therapy under the microscope, the more complex and rich matters become. Bob Michels (1985) observed, "The questions of what leads to change and when, are central to our work and are as yet unanswered" (p. 325). This is echoed by Arnold Cooper (1989) who notes, "It is consonant with our newer view of psychoanalysis that the question of how therapy works cannot be given a very satisfactory answer at this time" (p. 4).

Drs. Wolf and Settlage, in keeping with their interactional perspectives on the vicissitudes of development and on the factors that derail or arrest such development, have corresponding views on the therapeutic process. The language and the models they use are different, but as I read their chapters they both rather directly suggest that the locus of therapeutic action lies in the interaction between patient and analyst and that this interaction *in itself* is dominant in producing therapeutic change. Though neither author dismisses those components of analytic work that we usually consider of central importance, such as the lifting of repression, increasing self-knowledge, seeing new things about oneself, seeing old things in a new way, or augmenting self-analytic functioning, I was impressed that these factors did not seem of central importance to these authors as they formulated their perspectives of the psychoanalytic process.

Dr. Wolf points out that self psychology is not a monolithic theory. There were a number of shifts in Kohut's thinking and most certainly a conceptual spectrum among Kohut's students and colleagues. For instance, whereas Paul Ornstein seems to embrace both the self-understanding aspect of analytic therapy as well as the experience of empathic attunement in his concept of what cures, Arnold Goldberg and Robert Stolorow focus almost exclusively on the interactional component and on empathic attunement, which in themselves provide restorative selfobject experiences and ultimately psychic growth. I am not certain exactly where Dr. Wolf positions himself along this spectrum, although it is quite clear that from his perspective the interactional component—the patient feeling understood, efficacious, valued, and vitalized by the affective attunement with the analyst—plays a central role in the process of cure or restoration.

Dr. Settlage in discussing therapeutic action makes a distinction between disorders related to intrapsychic conflict and those deriving from developmental derailments. Parenthetically, I must comment that this distinction, which appears so clear on paper and in clinical extremes, becomes far more obscure in clinical practice. In the most recent volume of the *Journal of the American Psychoanalytic Association* (1993), Dr. Settlage makes this distinction with considerable clarity and sharpness in his theoretical discussion. However, when he then presents some very rich and detailed clinical material, these distinctions appear far more blurred. In addressing arrests in preoedipal development, Dr. Settlage, like Dr. Wolf, strongly advocates an interactional model of therapeutic intervention. He says that viewing the psychoanalytic relationship from the perspective of the interactional, developmental model of separation–individuation theory adds a new dimension to that of the traditional, noninteractional model geared to the resolution of pathology.

In analogy to the parents in child development, the analyst represents (a) an organizing influence; (b) a temporary auxiliary ego; (c) empathic understanding; (d) a safe and secure relationship; (e) respect and support for the patient's need for initiative, agency, and autonomy; (f) affirmation of the existing and emerging healthy sense of self. By behaving differently than the parent of childhood and not reinforcing the transference expectations, the analyst is furthering the undoing of pathology. At the same time, the different behavior makes the analyst suitable for developmental identification.

Nowhere in this description of the therapeutic process

does one read of uncovering repressed wishes or memories, clarifying or interpreting unconscious fantasies related to merger or abandonment, resolving intrapsychic conflict, and so forth. To illustrate the interactional aspect of the therapeutic process, Settlage outlines various principles of technique that he draws from the correlation of his observations on the child–parent interaction in the appeal cycle. Included in these principles of technique are (a) actively engaging the analytic relationship, (b) expressing empathy affectively and verbally, (c) encouraging and acknowledging developmental initiatives and achievements, and (d) offering and demonstrating availability when such clearly is needed.

My comments have been focused on a particular theme that runs through the chapters. I am left with many questions, a desire for greater clarity, and indeed some concern. It strikes me that in Dr. Wolf's chapter, in the propositions of self psychologists generally, and in Dr. Settlage's chapter, there is a shift in thinking that moves the interactional component to the foreground of the therapeutic arena. It appears that this shift in emphasis is subtly at the expense of what I see as our primary task in the psychoanalytic endeavor—trying to understand the inner world of our patients and somehow meaningfully conveying this understanding to them.

Dr. Levine in his study of Mahler's work, states that Mahler was quite clear "that the provision of a particular kind of growth-promoting relationship is only an adjunctive therapeutic factor in the analysis and so can never replace interpretation." I would go one step further: it seems to me that unless the therapeutic goal of increasing our understanding remains central in our thinking, we may well lose a firm grasp on the impact and meaning of the various and inevitable interactional components of our interventions. For instance, I wonder what it means to a child or adult who is struggling with impulse control to be "vitalized by affective attunement." Or, the impact on the child or adult struggling with fears of separation and abandonment to have the analyst "encourage developmental initiatives and achievements."

CONCLUSION

Powerful interactional elements are part of any and all meaningful human encounters. How could it be otherwise? Furthermore, an interactional component at some level is intrinsic to the efficacy of all treatment endeavors. However, it seems to me that unless our focus and primary effort is on trying to appreciate the inner world, the inner experience of our analysands, I am not sure how we can determine the meaning and impact of the interactional component, and if indeed such interaction is therapeutic.

I personally find a book such as this one rewarding and fulfilling, because new questions are raised and unexpected avenues for thought and exploration become evident. The three contributions, indeed the six contributions, have provided just such stimulation and richness, and I am personally most appreciative.

REFERENCES

Arieti, S. (1955). *Interpretation of Schizophrenia.* New York: Robert Brunner.

Casement, P. (1990). *Learning From The Patient.* New York: Guilford.

Cooper, A. M. (1989). Concepts of therapeutic effectiveness in psychoanalysis: a historical review. *Psychoanalytic Inquiry* 9:4–25.

Emde, R. N. (1980). Ways of thinking about new knowledge and further research from a developmental orientation. *Psychoanalysis and Contemporary Thought* 3:213–235.

Fischer, N. (1986). "Witch hunting": a form of reductionist thinking. *American Journal of Psychoanalysis* 46:45–54.

Jacobs, T. (1986). On countertransference enactments. *Journal of the American Psychoanalytic Association* 34:289–307.

Joseph, B. (1989). *Psychic Equilibrium and Psychic Change.* London: Tavistock/Routledge.

Lichtenberg, J. (1983). *Psychoanalysis and Infant Research.* Hillsdale, NJ: Analytic Press.

Lidz, T., and Fleck, S. (1960). Schizophrenia, human integration and the role of the family. In *The Etiology of Schizophrenia,* ed. D. Jackson, pp. 323–345. New York: Basic Books.

Marmor, J. (1983). Systems thinking in psychiatry: some theoretical and clinical implications. *American Journal of Psychiatry* 140:833–838.

Michels, R. (1985). The therapeutic action of psychoanalysis. *Contemporary Psychoanalysis* 21:320–325.

Papousek, H., and Papousek, M. (1983). Interactional failures: their origins and significance in infant psychiatry. In *Frontiers of Infant Psychiatry,* ed. J. D. Call, E. Galenson, and R. Tyson, pp. 276–283. New York: Basic Books.

Polansky, N. A., et al. (1981). *Damaged Parents: An Anatomy of Child Neglect.* Chicago: University of Chicago Press.

Rosen, N. (1953). *Direct Analysis—Selected Papers.* New York: Grune and Stratton.

Saul, L. J. (1980). *The Childhood Emotional Pattern and Psychodynamic Therapy.* New York: Van Nostrand Reinhold.

Settlage, C. (1993). Therapeutic process and developmental process in the restructuring of object and self constancy. *Journal of the American Psychoanalytic Association* 41:473–492.

Shapiro, T., and Stern, D. (1980). Psychoanalytic perspectives on the first year of life—the establishment of the object in an affective field. In *The Course of Life: Psychoanalytic Contributions Toward Understanding Personality Development,* vol. I, ed. S. I. Greenspan and G. H. Pollock, pp. 113–129. Washington, DC: National Institute of Mental Health.

Stern, D. (1985). *The Interpersonal World of the Infant.* New York: Basic Books.

Index